Ecology of Secrets

Arcadia Missa Publications

Unit 6 Bellenden Business Centre
Bellenden Road
Peckham
London
SE15 4RF

www.arcadiamissa.com
@ArcadiaMissa
info@arcadiamissa.com

Ecology of Secrets, 2013

ISBN: 978-0-9926747-1-7

With additional editing by Arcadia Missa and Felix L. Petty

Arcadia Missa Publications are available from the gallery and our website.

This publication has been kindly supported by the Arts Council England

LOTTERY FUNDED | Supported using public funding by ARTS COUNCIL ENGLAND

This book is printed in a limited edition of 100.
Signed by the author.

90 /100

Dorian Mode,

CHAPTER I: CHSTERTON

I'm writing to you about a project initiated by Scotland Yard called Operation CHSTERTON. It was meant to be named "Chesterton" apparently, but somebody failed to type in the first "e" and they just kept it that way so it wouldn't appear that they'd made a mistake. Sounds idiotic to you does it? Well, you're not the only one:

> From opdep1@syd.gov.uk
> To: tunnel1tunnel@syd.gov.uk
>
> Is this bollocks? Answer: Yes, Sir, it's bollocks. It looks like some chav-let's text message to his m8s about when they're going go smoke some melted offcuts from Legoland and bottle-rape a pensioner. Can you idiotz not tipe down n TUNEL OPS? Now I have to call this goat's scrotum of an operation CHSTERTON so that it doesn't look like you fuck ups are a load of fuck ups. How's that for deep fucking cover?
>
> I'm warning you, you lot of paedo birthday clowns, this type of thing happens again, heads will be ripped off, necks will be shat down.
>
> <3,
> Donald Justice

You'll recognise the name at the end of the message if nothing else. I'm sure you've seen his face on television, camera-ready but with his expression always poised between scowl and glower, Police Commissioner Donald Justice. I've seen him in person, it's the same expression but his epaulettes are less polished and he's always trying to find your eyes so that he can blink them into submission. He shook my hand three days after that email was sent and he told me I was in charge of a very important counter-terrorism operation. I was five years on the force, dedicated, loyal, and, I'd like to think, good at what I did. I'd worked on counter-terror operations for the last three years. I'd done some undercover work when I was in Drugs, but nothing prepared me for Operation CHSTERTON, they told me it would be the operation that would make me, define my career for the next thirty years. I'd be a legend on the force, they'd read about me in textbooks though probably not in the newspapers. Well, things never quite go the way you plan them to. This is the story of how I became one of the country's most dangerous terrorists after being one of its most trusted police officers.

It was just another sloshy spring Tuesday, I was sitting at my desk mechanically scrolling emails when I got called into the supervisor's office. He told me they had a big job for me. Deep cover. Very deep. Like earth's mantle deep. Maybe for years. He wanted to know if I was up for it.
"Absolutely, sir," I said.
"Of course you are. Just hope the rest of us are, too," he said.
He passed an envelope across his desk that had an index card inside. It was the number of a briefing room in Tunnel Ops. Around the offices, and the various punchbowls and snugs where coppers huddle, you heard all kinds of crazy stories about them, that they had people inside every important office in the country public and private, that they'd engineered the fall of RBS so that one of their operatives in senior management could leave without suspicion falling on them. They had people in Pakistan, Afghanistan, even the US, and that a Tunnel Ops guy was actually one of the royal footmen! In crazier versions he was the guy who read Prince Charles his bedtime story every night (*Patient Grizelda*, he'd had it read to him every single night since he was a baby and couldn't sleep without it, even now). When I walked down the hall to take the lift to the 9th floor to Tunnel Ops, all kinds of visions were running through my head. There I was in some dim warehouse in a shoot out, in the palace shielding the Duchess of Cambridge with my body. There I was, dropped from a helicopter into some tsetse fly colony in The Horn of Africa with only a few contacts' names in my head and a blade with another man's name on it. I was ready for anything.

I was told to go straight in. The head of Tunnel Ops (I can't write his name here without things becoming worse for me than they already are) told me that he'd been through my files and he'd noticed a few interesting bits of information. First, that I'd studied Earth Sciences at university.

"Bit unusual don't you think?"

"Unusual how, sir?"

"Like you're a bit 'save the arctic ocean', 'save the dolphins', 'save the bloody planet'."

"I'm not sure I follow, sir."

"Makes me think you might not be suited to the work we have for you."

"Again, I'm not entirely sure I'm fo--"

"It's a difficult climate out there. If you'll forgive my clever word-play. Who you trust and don't trust matters. Presently we trust you, well, most of us do. I'd just like to know where you stand on all this business."

"Business, sir?"

"The environment and all of that rubbish. You're not really one of these dreadlocked-canvas-bag-save-me-pubic-lice-shit-for-compost twats are you?"

"It's not a hairstyle I've ever considered sir."

"No, no I didn't think so. I thought there was more to you than that. I'm just worried there's too much more..."

He told me to sit down, he had something to show me.

It was the outline of the operation. Simple enough: an intelligence gathering operation that may involve what he termed "other dimensions". I was to set up a "cell" that purported to engage in environmental activism. Our aim was to get the UK to meet its carbon target projections as outlined under the Kyoto protocol. If possible, we wanted the government to actually curb emissions at a faster rate than required.

"If you'll excuse me, sir, isn't that official government policy as it is?"

He stopped pointing to the Power Point bullets.

"See, it's talk just like that that concerns me. Makes me think I'm taking a gamble I shouldn't be taking."

"Sir, you can trust me. I suppose I'm just wondering where my group would figure in things if the government is more or less in agreement with us."
"Policies change," he said.
I sat quietly for the rest of the presentation.
I was to recruit other officers to the cell and we'd work out of a house in Clarence Road in Hackney which we were supposed to be "squatting" but which the Yard had bought for the operation shortly after the Climate Camp protests.
"There's actually some rubbish in there we need to clear at the moment, but you'll move in at the weekend. We want you to break in properly. Messy. Noise and all that. Saturday is D-Day. Your calendar clear?"
"It is now, sir."
The rest of the project was standard intelligence work, we'd set out to make connections with as many groups in the area, and nationally, as possible, then we'd wait for orders.
"When I say 'orders' I don't mean that there will always be a 'do this do that' about the operation, you'll have considerable scope for shall we say, blue-sky thinking. One of your lot will be looking after your day-to-day. I call him Unholy Fuck Nut. The PM calls him Justice. You'll call him 'Blackbird'."
"Sounds like what I've been waiting for, sir."

In the paper the following morning I read about the rubbish clearing. Latvians. They'd been squatting the place for the last four months. They were dragged out of the house and, conveniently, found to be dealing drugs and swiftly processed by HM Border and Customs service with the requisite speed and sharpness their crimes demanded.

My first problem was putting together my "cell". Maximum ten people, ideal number six, both in terms of budgeting and for keeping the circle tight.
"Won't be the fucking Pewter Jubilee if this shit ends up in the papers."

I thought the best way to make my cell as believable as

possible was to recruit officers who had already had a few run-ins with the brass. I figured they'd be able to provide the kind of authenticity Tunnel Ops wanted. I met Raymond Carter when I was working Drugs. He was the same age as me, black, not particularly distinguished by radicalism, but there was an incident during a stop and search out on the Marshes that bothered him. His partner got a little too entertained by tasering a kid and the kid had some kind of heart thing. He didn't die, but it was close. Raymond wasn't exactly comfortable with the incident report and he let a few too many people know about it. He decided to pursue other career pathways last summer. I rang him up and told him about the job.

"I'm enjoying my retirement."

"Where are you working now?"

"Skating rink. Security meat puppet."

"We need you."

"That wasn't the feeling I got."

"Well, this is different, I need you. Okay?"

"No."

"I've been holding out on you. There's another part of the job. You'll like it. Besides, you're too talented to be a rent-a-cop."

"I *like* George Clinton."

"Let's just say no one will arrest you for affray with a police officer, should the occasion arise, and Raymond, I have a funny feeling it will.

"And no one will arrest them for affray with a nigger, if I remember correctly."

"Look this is intelligence work. It could lead places. Government work."

I knew Raymond had a thing for John LeCarré and if I dangled the spectre of spooks in front of him, immoveable objects might just turn out to have been incorrectly classified. He didn't say anything for a long time. I heard the sound of his street, lorries reversing, kids shouting from a basketball court cum football pitch. I knew he was still listening.

"How long would this little performance last if you don't mind my asking?"

Raymond was quiet, but I knew the longer he took to answer the surer the answer was. He was onboard. But Raymond was only part of the picture. We needed youth, we needed diversity, we needed sex appeal. We needed a woman.

I thought I had just the lady for the job in Anna Farthington. I knew her a bit and had heard she already belonged to some kind of environmental group as it was, so that was most of the battle, or so I thought. I told her about the project and you'd think I'd asked her to come over and cook me a full English. "See you in hell," was the only thing she said. I tried two other young juniors but they were such shit actors they'll probably be on The Bill next season. I was getting worried that the circle was looking a little too expansive. With the two kids I'd pulled from down in narcotics, Alex and Paul, I had a four person team plus the three rejections, then I found Martha.

Martha had been a PC for three years, Raymond suggested that I talk to her when I kept running into walls and aggro.
"She's hardcore, mate. Just look at her right arm."
That's not the kind of line that exactly inspires confidence in me, I don't know about you, still I was running out of ideas so I set up an appointment at my office, or rather my squat. When she turned up, I saw what Raymond meant. Her right arm was one massive tattoo, it's hard to describe exactly what the tattoo depicted. It made her arm look like it was covered in some kind of reptilian skin, only there was a lot of shaggy hair drawn on around the forearm. I tried not to stare but when you go to shake someone's hand, well, it's hard to avoid not noticing something like that. I gave her a cup of tea, some of the new ayurvedic bollocks the people from the office issued me with, and I asked her to sit down on one of the beanbags I'd picked up from a skip. She smiled and crossed her legs and sat right in the middle of the least-stained one. I sat across from her on the one I'd dubbed "the red blood cell". Okay, I said, the project I wanted to talk to about was a little bit unusual.
"For instance, these aren't my dreadlocks," I said, holding the crappy implants I'd been fitted with and shaking them, "That's obviously your tattoo though, right?"

"I paid for it."
"What's it of if you don't mind my asking?"
"It's Grendel's arm."
"Grendel? What's that?"
"You know, Beowulf."
"Oh, of course, yeah, Beowulf. Sorry."
"I've got another one," she said, and she undid the top buttons of the blouse she was wearing, it was a big black arrow pointing up from her chest to her face and it said, "Meet Grendel's Mother."
"Nice," I said.
"I like it," she said.
"I'll tell you a little about the operation, if you think it's the kind of thing you can handle, we could certainly use another person." I told her the ins and outs. She said it was right up her street, when could she start.
I told her it wasn't all fun and games, she had to remember it was serious intelligence work. She nodded from time to time to let me know she was following me, but I had to make sure she knew the whole story, the risks, the dangers.
"The thing is, there could be times when things get violent." She arched her eyebrows and started undoing the next few buttons on her blouse. She stood up and walked my way. My mind was racing, I had no idea what she was expecting me to do, or what she was expecting to do to me.
"Look close," she said.
She had a massive swordfish tattooed on her stomach, it stretched from just beneath her ribs to down past her knickers to her leg, the tail fins were invisible but underneath the scales and the added sea-splash, there were three unmistakable bullet wounds just underneath her ribcage.
"2011. An Essex car park. I'm a mule but I'm also a mole. They got suspicious and decided to cut their losses." I'd heard the story of that raid, it was a bit of a legend, but I just assumed the officer involved did the sane thing and returned to civilian life with a decent disability pension from a grateful country. My worries were over.
"I can handle risks," she said, and put her top back on.

Chapter II: Another Name, Another Face, Another Haircut

Since I made my decision to blow the whistle, I've thought a lot about what it means to be a spy. The ethics, the logic. I didn't give it much thought when I started out, for me it was all one big adventure, I didn't spend a lot of Sunday afternoons wondering about whether what I was doing was right. I was a police officer, how could I be doing something wrong? I stood with the law behind me; the public were the problem, the ones who wanted to damage and disrupt, to drain the marrow from the bones of society, to make us weak, brittle and powerless, vulnerable to the slightest push. It was true that I was the one in the shadows, living under an assumed name, the name, it turns out of a child who was run over by a lorry in 1979. It was policy in the department to use the names of dead people, preferably children, they wouldn't complain and besides, we thought, it makes things a little bit muddier if someone gets curious on Google search. Like the street sweepers and the people who run shelters, sometimes you have to work in the dark so that society can function during the daytime. I saw myself as the security guard at a building called society.

People outside the world of policing and intelligence work see spying as something totally alien, a thing apart from the values they understand, an island of dead letter boxes and fake beards, stilettos and poison. When you work inside you see that it's really part of an ecology, an ecology of secrets. When most people look at the world, they see what's "there", surfaces, people walking, the sky, trees, but that's such a tiny part of the reality that it doesn't even merit comment. Maybe it's my training, but when I see these things, buildings, houses, even people, what strikes me isn't what I see, but what I don't see, how much is concealed. Everyone has secrets, everyone devises strategies to keep them hidden. Every time you meet someone it's a delicate process of give and take, you can see it when you speak to people at parties or at work, in their eyes there's this little bit of scrutiny when they talk to you, what can I tell you, what should I hold back. Women will understand what I mean instinctively, in every purse I've ever inspected, I find a little tube of "concealer". Every office hides a backroom, every house hides a bedroom and a bathroom and a closet where we keep our junk, our skeletons and our true selves. It's the same in nature, too, from squirrels squirreling things away to ferrets ferreting them out. Everyone spies. To look at the world and see that for the first time, to see it and to understand what it means about everything we do or say, then you begin to understand. What we do is just a formal version of a very basic instinct. The question isn't *will* you spy, it's how and when. And for me, for us, our cell, it was about spying because we felt what we were doing was right and necessary, that it served a larger purpose than just finding a stash of acorns in a hollowed-out log. It was a way of keeping society safe. In a way, I saw what we were doing as work *against* spying. If we did our jobs, our society stayed as free and open as possible in the face of threats.

That's what I told myself. At first it was enough. Besides, there were enough logistical problems to keep us busy. We had to "re-take" the squat, for instance. Once the Latvians were cleared away, the force was very careful to install proper security and locks on the place and to put up loads of signs warning that trespassers would be prosecuted to the fullest extent of the law by the owners and, God willing, beyond that. We agreed that we'd go in on a Wednesday morning at 3AM in March, just warm enough, just late enough, just dead enough.

It wasn't as hard as we'd expected. The door was deadbolted but we sliced a section out of a ground floor window and went in. They'd actually alarmed the place which was problematic, but Raymond earned his pay cheque by disabling it before any lights in the neighbouring houses went on. As far as they were concerned it was just another stray car alarm on some arsehole's BMW. Inside, the place was actually quite nice. The Latvians were chucked out in a daylight raid and weren't allowed to take more than a single bag of personal effects with them. This was lucky for us because there were beds and furniture, some tea in the kitchen, and a TV. "Make sure we're not paying the TV license on that thing," Raymond said.

I told the young guys from narco to go in the kitchen and make tea for us.
"Have you seen this," Martha asked shining her torch into one of the little rooms down the hall. The room was full of children's things, a cradle and a couple of little electronics and a xylophone. I took a look. Obviously I didn't feel good about it, but in the situation we were in there wasn't much time to reflect on the rights or wrongs of what our Latvian predecessors had dealt with. I told her to put it all in a bin liner and I'd take it down to the charity shop in Stoke Newington first thing in the morning.

It was late, but none of us were tired. I think we still had a bit of a buzz going from the break in, so we all sat down in the living room, drank our tea and talked about what we were going to do with the place. One of the young guys, Pete Allen (d. 1986, aged 11 in a boating accident), had the best idea.
"I've been thinking it through, sir,"
"I told you not to call me sir, my name's Brendan O'Herlihy," I said. (d. 1991, aged 4 months, cot death), "Better yet, let's just come up with something, we all need nicknames, so call me, I don't bloody know, 'Spanx'. Yeah, call me Spanx."
"Spanks with a 'k, s' or Spanx with an 'x'," Raymond asked.
"With an 'x'. Now get on with it, Sneaky Pete."
"I was thinking, Spanx, it might make sense to use the place as a kind of community centre of some kind, you know? Literacy classes, use the back garden to grow veg that sort of thing. That way people will come round, we can crowdsource..."
"That's a good idea."
"What the fuck is crowdsourcing?" Raymond asked.
"It means to use the intel they give us to structure campaigns. For example, say they're worried about some school closing or something like that, we can stage demos or," Pete looked to me for approval, "interventions based on what the community tells us."
"I like it, Sneaky Pete."
"Thanks, Spanx."
"No problem. We're going to need to vote on this, all in

favour raise your hands."
Everyone raised a hand except Raymond.
"Is there a problem Tank?"
"Tank?"
"That's your nickname."
Spanx, Tank, going through the alphabet, mate? Not gonna be pretty when he gets to you Gavs."
"If you don't like it change it now so we get it all straight from the start."
"To what Bradley Fighting-Vehicle? Tank it bloody is. Tanks a bloody lot. Is this shit, any of it, even legal, Captain Spanx?"
"Tank, it's all good, trust me on this. We're covered."
"Covered? Shit, more like buried."
Raymond, or Tank, took a drink from his tea and shook his head and raised his hand. Game on.

The first few months everything worked like a charm, but there was one problem and according to the directors of the operation back at Tunnel Ops, it was serious one. Though we were sending them piles and piles of data, they weren't finding anything that was actually illegal. I had meetings with Justice/ Blackbird every two weeks. I would pretend to go skip diving, I was running a line promoting freeganism to people who came by the squat, or Newer Grange as we'd started calling it. He'd pick me up a few blocks from the squat and we'd drive out through Hackney to the marshes and talk there.
"It's the friendly rats in the Tunnel. They're not entirely happy with things."
"What does 'not entirely' mean?"
"It means you send us a load of data about old ladies thinking library closings are the worst thing since Genghis Khan with the clap and how some kids want to open up a bloody skate park and you think you're doing your job? That's what 'not bloody entirely' means."
"I can only tell you what they tell us."
"That's not good enough. I don't know what you think this is? Some kind of Am Dram happening where you lot sit around listening to psychedelic classics for a year and smoke

a lot of e-joints until we call you back to the office and pin an OBE on your nipple piercing, it's intelligence work. That word 'work', it has a meaning. It doesn't mean giving bloody English lessons to refugees as our deceased friend Peter has developed a passion for."

"It would help if you were more specific about the outcomes."

"Specificity you want? Okay then, we need actionable intelligence. We're getting inaction and stupidity. We've got a budget you know, and there's lots of little quinoa farting PPE genital warts up in Chancery Lane who'd like nothing better than to get out the pink-o shears and give us a right royal snip round the urethra. I have to go to meetings, too, you know, only they're not with intrepid, handsome officers of the peace, they're with pus balls in pinstripes who go to the electorate every now and again and want to look like George Bloody Smiley. I need scalps and I need them quick and you're going to get your tomahawk out or I'll put some serious sphincter disabling dread into your dreadlocks."

He drove me back to a skip a few blocks from the squat. I got out of the car. He put up two fingers as a kind of goodbye then he moved them together like scissors.

Our involvement in direct action was an outgrowth of that conversation. Again, I'm not proud of what I was involved in, but I think, looking back on it now, I'm glad we had that discussion. It led to OPERATION AHAB which, now, in the fullness of time I consider to be the most worthwhile thing I've done with my life.

Chapter III: The Whale Finds AHAB

Operation AHAB began by accident. I was working with Martha, who was now named Lilith (d. 1984, aged 15, meningitis) on what we'd planned to be our big operation, a protest at a Bank of England interest rate meeting. I was reading a story about quantitative easing on the BBC's website when a news flash at the top of the page started going nuts: *"REPORTS FROM CORNWALL SUGGEST A SPERM WHALE HAS BEACHED NEAR NEWQUAY"*. The report included a quote from a scientist who said that he thought the beaching might be a result of British naval operations in the North Sea, that the sonar used by our submarines might have been driving whales into unfamiliar waterways where they get lost and end up dying. It struck me as an incredible opportunity, like the universe was handing me the kind of operation we needed on a silver platter.

"Lilith, come over and have a look at this."

She read the story.

"It sounds terrible."

"What? Oh, yeah, no it does sound terrible. I mean I'd hate to be that whale," I assumed she was in character when she'd said what she said and so I decided to see if I could make the operation happen entirely without breaking character.

"Fucking crime is what it is. Imagine that, you're just a whale up in the North Sea or wherever you live and you're out there working on your song, looking for some krill or plankton or something and all you can hear is this deafening bloody sonar drowning out everything. Screeeeech! After a while it starts making your crazy and then, what the fuck, you're in Bermondsey! Fuck me. I mean, really, fuck me. You know what we should do?"

"What?"

"I mean, we can't just sit by and watch shit like this. We should go down there, down to Cornwall. We should stage a protest."

Lilith looked at me somewhat puzzled at first, but then I think she caught my meaning.

"That could work," she said.

"We need a house General Assembly. Now!"

I texted Sneaky Peter, Tank and Sneaky Gavin and told them to be back at the squat within the hour. Our mission had found us.

The next person I spoke to was Blackbird. When I told him about the plan he was over the moon. Over the moon and halfway through the Van Allen asteroid belt.

"Gooood lad, just like they tell you down in Soho. So it's torches and crusties dancing round a whale is it? Shame I can't join you. What happens next then?"

"Next?"

"Yeah, like next, you know like bloody NEXT after your little handshake with the universe. What comes next? What's the pay-off?"

I hadn't fully thought it through, but I told him we were meeting to talk about it this afternoon, but I assumed it would involve the carcass somehow.

"I don't know yet. I'll get back to you. Just make sure nothing happens to that whale until we get there."

"Roger the bloody cabin boy."

A few minutes later everyone arrived. It had been a productive day kerb crawling. Peter wanted to log in some of the data he'd collected from the fake bike clinic he'd set up near London Fields ("People will tell you their whole life story if you have a cycle pump, Spanx").

"This is an emergency. Everything has to wait."

"What is all this, DEFCON 1 bullshit?" Tank asked. He wasn't happy, but then he wasn't usually happy, not least with the job I'd given him running a rasta stall in Ridley Road Market. Mostly it was just locals who hung around his shop asking him for drugs. He never reported them. I looked him straight in the face.

"It's the biggest thing you've ever seen."

It involved a bit of horsetrading, but eventually they all came around. Operation AHAB was on the move from 1800 hours that evening. The plan was simple enough. I say simple, but some parts were simpler than others. The basic idea was that we would "liberate" the whale carcass from the beach using hardware from the office. We'd transport the dead whale to a power station in Dungeness and grab some headlines along the way. I gave Blackbird the full story.

"Well, I'll be straight with you, lad, unlike your gym teachers were. Carry On Carrion up the M1's not going to be easy," he paused, breathed in and said, "Scratch that. It's not going to happen, not as you see it."

"Where's the problem?"

"Well, look, it's not exactly easy-peasy-sperm-whale-squeezy to move a dead whale out of Cornwall without anybody noticing is it? We'd have to call in MOD to get that kind of hardware, if not the Americans. Personnel, logistics, you're looking at a couple of million quid down the pan at that point, not to mention the suspicions it would raise to help you lot score a Hercules to help with the old heave-ho. Moby Dick's going to need a little more than herbal Viagra to get him up."

I took his point, but I just thought of the optics it would generate, that whale strung up from a smokestack. I had to make it happen.

"What about a flatbed," I asked.

"Appeals to certain kinds of women, some prefer the kitchen table, why?"

"Look if we get a flatbed, all we'll need is personnel. I think with the contacts we've generated over the last months, I think we could make this happen. I'm serious."

"I get that. Look, you little dam building marine mammal you, what we can give you is money and maybe some armour from the stockpile, but this is high risk low reward. If I wanted to gamble I'd be down with me nephew Sean at Paddy Power betting on flies at the piss trough."

"It's not low reward. Think of how many people you could scoop up if we get everyone we know involved? It's at least trespassing, I'd think."

"I like it but I don't like it. I can get you five k, maybe another 5k on spec, but you're on your own here, you cock it up, it's your cock, you get me?"

We were in complete overdrive from the end of that call. Tank designed a leaflet to be handed out and we ran off about a hundred copies and gave them to Sneaky Pete and Lilith. I sent them to Cecilia Road and Clarence Road hoping we could count on at least the two eco-squats there. I told them also to hang around Broadway Market and if anyone "looked sympathetic" to sound them out about getting involved. "This means anybody playing the digeridoo, anybody juggling. Dreadlocks are a judgement call and tattoos are not to be considered sufficient evidence for approach. Tattoos must either be tribal in appearance, involve marijuana leaves or Arabic script."

I told Tank to monitor the email and be in touch if anything came up. I couldn't risk him on the streets in an operation as crucial as this because of the stop-and-search regime on the go in Hackney at the time. A black man handing out literature in the streets was guaranteed to attract attention from all the wrong people.

I ran as fast as I could to the nearest cash point to make sure our funds were in the account. Then I got on Gumtree to see about hiring a flatbed. The only place that had a truck the size we needed was out in Leyton. It was run by a guy called "Mad" Mick McGillis who sounded from the advert like he might be ex-military. I thought it might complicate things, but I didn't have a choice. Text messages were coming in from Lilith that the Cecilia Road squat was onboard. I got a text from the guy who organised the squat, called himself "Tomrade Number One" "This is so fucking *money*, man. See you in Newquay/Hell!"

I rang Tank and told him he was in charge of affairs until I got back. I jumped into the tube and headed out to Leyton.

Chapter IV: Secret Services

Mad Mick's place was in a row of warehouses on an industrial estate that the last twenty years forgot. He was sitting in a lawn chair with a styrofoam cup of tea reading the Daily Sport when I found him. He put down his paper, looked me over and stood up at a kind of faded attention.
"Looking for anyone particular, guv?"
"Mad Mick?"
"The very bowels," he reached out to shake my hand and did his best to crush it.
"I need to hire some hardware."
"I can show you Long Meg out the back, indeed I can, but if you don't mind my asking, guv. What may I ask do you expect to be transporting on my fair lady?"
"Farming equipment, quite a lot."
"Lumber?"
"Bit of lumber. Quite a bit actually."
"Lumber in London? Blimey, guv, that's a new one. I've been to Forest Gate meself, bit of a disappointment, really. No forest. No gate either. Who exactly do they think they're kidding?"
"Actually we're hauling the lumber into the Smoke, mate. Going to be a long drive."
"The Charles Dickens you say. And where are you moving this lumber from? Not from beyond our fair shores I hope."
"Wales actually."
"Ah, yes. The Welsh forests. Look, guv," he said, taking a step closer to my face, "don't know what you think of a fella like me, out here in the bloody sticks, or the bricks as it were, stashed among the pricks, as it always is, but I didn't just fall off the flatbed lorry last Tuesday. I gave old Galtieri what was what, when it was my time, and I got too much metal in me leg for you to be yanking it thus. What the fuck do you want me flatbed for, you pissabed palm tree with your bloody reggae ropes bouncing all round? I'm not going out of business so you can set up a rave in bloody Beddegelert thank you very much. And if you think you're going to transport drugs on my bloody property, well, lad, the two of us are going to have to have a discussion."

He hitched up his trousers and fixed his eyes on me with as much menace as he could. I looked down into his sun-stained, meaty face as it twitched with readiness for a little post-Argie Argie Bargy and told him I couldn't tell him what I needed Long Meg for but that I respected that he'd answered the call of duty when it came, and that I hoped he'd recognise it now, even after all these years, when it came again. He looked me over again, then his face softened, or at least I think it did, he may have just been preparing to break my knees.

"On Her Majesty's Secret Service are we? A cause close to me own heart. Won't mind paying a bit more for your troubles then, will you?"

"It sounds like you understand my predicament, Mick."

"That's Mad Mick, mate. Mad. Mick. Don't put it on the business cards to amuse meself."

"Of course, Mad Mick."

"Say 3k for the weekend suit you?"

"Let's say three five."

"I knew there was something I liked about you, lad. Can see it in how you carry yourself."

As I drove away Mad Mick gave me a sharp salute which I returned with as much crispness as I could muster. Game on.

We went down to Newquay in a convoy. In the flatbed it was Tank and me. Lilith rode with people from the Clarence House squat and Gavin with the Cecilia Road people, and Sneaky Pete was sent on a mission to scoop up as many of both groups' interested friends as he could. We set out from London at 8.30 hoping to reach New Quay in the dead of night and drive it straight through so that we were back in London just after first light. As I took Long Meg out on the motorway it dawned on me that there would be at least one big problem to deal with and that was the fact that everyone in the country would be looking for a whale carcass when it was found to be missing and once we had it; it wasn't going to be easy to hide. I tasked Raymond with finding us a secure facility. I told him to call Blackbird, they'd have somewhere. I was sure of that.

I could hear Blackbird on Tank's mobile. He was in a good mood.
"I wish I could be out there with you lads, and that's not just because Duncan from Narcotics is blowing me now and he hasn't bloody flossed, unlike last time! Have you thought what you're going to do with the old tramps knacker yet?"
"At the moment we're looking for a place to put it. I was thinking hide it in plain sight but I don't want us to get in trouble for running an unlicensed fish stand in Hackney. I understand they get testy about those things. Could blow our cover."
"Look, this is a special occasion. Not everyone knows about a little space we keep in South London for just such emergencies. I'll give you the post code."
Tank checked the incoming text.
"SW8 5BP," Tank said, "Why does that sound familiar?"
It took a minute to click, but then I remembered.
"It's Battersea Power Station."
"Batter... you mean, *we* run it?"
"Apparently."
"How we going to explain that to our friends in the magic bus back there?"
I felt a wave of dread sweep over me, then it came to me like a bolt out of the blue.
"No, we don't explain, that's the operation. We stage a break in. We buy steel cables and we hang the whale outside the station. That's it. It's gorgeous."
"Maybe you'd better let me drive," Tank said.

Chapter V: The Beach

I'd never been to Newquay before. I'd never actually been to Cornwall. I thought it would be just another sleepy little village plucked straight from my imagination; rocks, waves, seabirds spiraling out over the white froth. I wasn't ready for the reality. First, there were police everywhere. We drove in on the M5 and we could see police wagons everywhere on the streets in the town.
"Do they know we're coming," Gavin asked.
"Of course they know we're coming," I said.
"Yeah, but do they know we're us," Tank said.
"Some of them," I said.
I drove the flatbed up Trevemper Road and tried to find a place where it wouldn't be conspicuous. It wasn't easy and so we ended up driving for nearly an hour until we found a row of warehouses out past a camping ground.
"This is going to have to do for now. We'll walk into the town," I said. Blackbird gave me sticker for the window when he gave us the van so that there wouldn't be issues if any police got suspicious. I put it in the window of the truck and hoped for the best.
"Let's see what this is all about," I said.
I want to be very clear about the fact that I'm not boasting here, but I've done some dangerous police work in my time. I've been on raids, I've been involved in cover operations. I've been shot at twice and I've had three blokes ready to tear my head off after some football violence in West Ham, but I've never felt in more danger than I did that day in Newquay. The city was like something out of a film, a load of teenage yob zombies taking over an entire village, everywhere you turned there were kids drinking, yelling at each other across pavements, honking horns, blowing those bloody vuvuzela things.
"What the fuck is this? Some kind of hippy Glastonbury thing?"
"It's end of term."
"Fucking more like end of civilisation."
I watched a kid hanging on to the roof of a van with what looked like a Chewbacca mask on his head. Police saw him and their cars shrieked into action and tailed them round the

corner. The kid went headfirst down the sunroof of the van. Last I saw him, his legs were still hanging out the roof as our boys followed them round a bend in the road toward some kind of occult shop.
"This isn't going to make things any easier."
By now I'd gotten texts from the other squat guys from London. They'd found places to park and were heading our way. I told them to meet us on the beach and to be careful.

As you can imagine, the fact that a whale was washed up on Fistral Beach wasn't exactly lost on the end of term army. When we got to the beach it was probably 2AM. There was something like a rave going on on one side of the bay, a massive bonfire was lit and kids were jumping all around listening to some Dubstep shit.
"Fancy Moby Dick washed up next to a load of dicks listening to Moby," Tank said, "Police work, innit, Spanx."
In the light from the fire we could see the whale. It was gigantic. Far bigger than it had looked on the internet. It was like a massive grey cloud that fell to earth and settled on the dark shore. The firelight seemed to almost create a kind of aura around the whale, as if someone were running an electrical current through it. My heart was already pounding. The police had set up a couple of rows of fencing around the whale's carcass and there was a group of guards on duty. Little groups had also gathered around the police cordon, druids from the look of them, some of them nearly naked, all wearing seaweed crowns in their hair. I thought of them as our allies, but they'd have to be convinced. It wasn't going to be a clean or easy. I sent Peter and Gavin to sound out the kids at the rave about the general story. I figured we had about three hours before people started to pass out or enter catatonic states from the horse paralyzers and medical waste or whatever it was they'd be taking now that their GCSE English exams were over. The police presence looked light, but we were going to have to make it lighter. I was sure there'd be a few teams sitting around reading The Sun waiting for things to kick off as they inevitably would. We had to make sure they kicked off downbeach to let us have a

shot. I sent Lilith and Tank off for a "night stroll" around the perimeter of the beach to see if they saw any of our co-workers in evidence nearby. I was thinking that I should have brought some of the flash-bang grenades I'd gotten from Tunnel Ops when they inspected the squat and told us we needed some "housewarming" presents. Before I could gather my thoughts, Tomrade slapped me on the back.
"Yo, Spanx, I saw the profile, knew it couldn't be anyone else. Him a natty, natty dread man!"
"Tomrade!"
"Looks like they've got old Moby sky-kettled. This is just the beginning," he said, motioning to the cordon around the whale. I saw a couple of wagon loads of 'em back toward the camping grounds getting suited and bruted. They've got something up the sleeves of their body armour, no bank-bailout about it." Tomrade's "99% rhyming slang" was the last thing I was in the mood for. Hearing there was a whole other deployment on the way down to the beach meant I was going to have to be much more creative. A diversion would only divert part of them. Then, out of nowhere, Tomrade earned his keep. He was staring out at the rave and at the black and gold smear of the water. "Shit, mate, the only way I can think of getting in there is to pretend we're fuzz too. You John Peel me?" Tomrade was laughing in his joyful, emphysemic way, but he was right; it was the perfect solution. Coppers pretending to be activists pretending to be coppers.

I rallied the troops. We met down beach in the long, shadows of the rave bonfire. Tomrade was going on about the Manu Chau gig he wanted to see when we got back to London, but my mind was nearing lightspeed, making, then scrapping, plans of action. Sneaky Pete and Sneaky Gavin turned up late, it looked like they were having fun. Peter had a glow stick that he was playing with. I told him to stop unless he wanted it to become a suppository. There was no hope of doing anything tonight.
"This beach has more fuzz than hippie pussy," I said.
Tomrade laughed again and said, "That shit's *wrong*, mate.

Funny as fuck, but *wrong*!"

"We're going to have to set up camp," Tank said.

I agreed and told them I'd hit them with a plan in the morning.

"So, tonight, chillax, smoke up, make friends. We're on the clock from 0500."

"Where you going, Spanxy?"

"Gotta ring a friend, we're going to need someone with a little bit of parking space when we get back."

I watched them all head into the rave except for Lilith who settled in with the druids. She was bloody good.

I walked up toward the cliffs away from the city and rang Blackbird.

"Bit late isn't it, Queequeg?"

"There's been a snag."

"What's the matter, todger stuck in the blowhole?"

"It's our guys. They're everywhere. There's some kind of end of term orgy going on here too. We're having to think outside the box."

"Or the aquarium as it were."

"I've got a plan. But it may get complicated. We may need I.T. I think we might have to break into some computers. We're thinking of running double cover."

"Bit warm for double covers don't you think?"

I gave him a quick synopsis of the plan I'd thrown together. We were going to go all the way, blow the budget. We were going to get the whale in broad daylight tomorrow. We were going to pretend to be from CEFAS (The Centre for Environment Fisheries and Acquaculture Sciences, if you didn't already know), say we're going work with the MOD and we need the carcass for science *tout suite*, nobody can know. Clear the beach etc. But we were going to need credentials. "I'm thinking I'm going to need to get into somebody at CEFAS's official email so that 'he' can write to the police here."

"Why didn't you just say so? You could have at least let me get through the Juno Temple dream I was having. You know the one where she kind of gives you this snotty little teenager look while you're fucking her from behind? But you probably don't

have that one, do you, Spanxy boy. With you, it's Prezza in a French maid outfit. Give me twenty minutes."
Blackbird hung up and I sat on the cliff's edge and looked down on the beach. The people were coming and going. From where I was you could only just see the bonfire, hear the boom of the speakers, see long black streak that was the whale. I was buzzing with excitement, but I couldn't help thinking of all the kids down there, dancing around, celebrating the end of term next to this massive dead whale. It was a vision of a nightmare future. What would next season be like? Whales laid out up and down the beach, kids turning their bodies into stages, Fatboy Slim or the fucking Chemical Brothers stringing them all up and doing a lightshow on their bodies... it didn't bear thinking about. My "office" mobile rang. "Ahoy, then, Ish-she/male, you're now Professor Jonas Higgins of CEFAS' lead cetacean research team. At least until he finds out, which he won't because the orcs in IT are on the job and I've got somebody from the department dropping round his house in the morning to make sure he doesn't get to the bottom of his bowl of bloody granola until after dinner Cornwall time. Your password is "uNfr33w1lly". Also, I've booked you lot two rooms at the Gannet B&B so you've got a place to work out of. I don't need to tell you we have an arrangement with the proprietors. I'm texting you the address now. Now get to fucking work and let me fucking sleep."

I headed down to the beach to catch up with everyone. The crowd seemed to have grown even larger, more dense, one of those English crowds where you feel absolutely anything could happen, like the entire social and political mentality of the mob could change at the flick of a switch. In one context they'd be grooving to reggae and listening to somebody sing about how the police should be killed and we were all one, yet if somebody started talking about British jobs for British workers there'd be cheers just as loud.

Some gig must have let out, or an entire pub must have been evacuated for violating its tosser occupancy limit, because it

was like riding the tube at rush hour now; I tried to cut a path through the sweat and beer and sea breeze. I invented a little game with myself to keep from going insane or from reverting to my crowd control training and blowing the whole operation. When I got a fix on a particular face, I'd try to guess from their look what they'd been studying at university. For the guys, denim shorts meant left wing chemists, collared shirts denoted business studies or marketing, depending on the hair cut. A beard was meaningless unless wedded to other characteristics, for example, moccasins meant literature, and sandals Eastern studies. With the women, dreadlocks almost always meant history or anthropology. Preppy girls I decided were art history or modern languages. One girl had a septum ring and I could see a massive yin-yang tattoo between her breasts. She could've been local. I was trying to figure out if a guy with tribal tattoos on his arm and expensive shades was just an MBA in waiting who was trying too hard or a conservatory jazz student with rich parents when I felt someone tap me on the shoulder. I assumed it was one of the crew but, no, it was a girl, probably about twenty-three in one of those floppy gypsy dresses with a long braid that twisted round her head like a halo.
"What's your name," she called over the periodic bass thuds.
"Er, Spanx. How about you?"
"Spanx! That's cute."
"Yeah. What's your name?"
"Psyche."
"Nice name."
"Yeah. Hippie Oxford parents. What are you up to. You down here to surf?"
"Surf? No, why?"
"You look a little like a surfer."
"No, just visiting friends."
"Where're your friends?"
"I got lost. Had to take a call and went up to the cliff up there. No idea where they're at now."
"It's a nice cliff."
"Yeah. Where are you from?"
"Oxford."

"That where you study?"
"No, SOAS. You know it?"
"Yeah. I live in London."
"Oh yeah?"
"I've got a squat in Dalston. You know it?"
"Yeah, didn't there used to be some Latvian people squatting down there? You living with them?"
"I don't know about any Latvians. When we got there it was empty."
"That's weird. There was a place with some Latvians down there. You guys might be neighbours. Maris is really cool. He fixes bikes."
"Might be. What brings you down here?"
"Oh, you know, partying. And the whale thing. I wanted to see it."
"It's incredible."
"It's fucked. We're fucking everything up. We're just taking a shit into the ocean and expecting to get a fucking medal for it."
"No. I mean, yeah, it's totally true."
"So you been in the scene long?"
"Scene?"
"Squatting. I know a lot of people in the scene. We've probably got some friends in common."
"Well, not really, not in England. I've been, uh, living abroad for a while."
"Cool, where?"
"Uh well, Nicaragua, actually."
"That's so fucking sick, do you know Spydrew? Tall guy, lots of ink, wears a shark tooth necklace all the time? He was living in a forest community down there. He's really fucking cool."
"Didn't meet him. I was working on a project with some campesinos. Just outside the capital, so kind of more of an urban vibe, you know?"
I was praying she wasn't going to ask me what the capital of Nicaragua was.
"Sounds cool," was all she said.

I told her I was looking for my friends and she told me she'd lost her friends, too.
"Maybe if we hang out together we'll find them together," she said.
I was so deep in the operation, I couldn't decide if having her around was a good or bad thing. In one sense, she was exactly the kind of person I was on Operation CHSTERTON to meet, an internationally-connected British citizen who, according to the guidelines we had, we could easily classify as a "domestic extremist". Her scalp would be worth something, though how much it was difficult to tell. From the perspective of Operation AHAB, she might offer another pair of hands, but then she might also add just the kind of inefficiency we didn't need. If word got out, not that it would from me, but maybe from Tank of the Sneakies if they were deep cover and smoking or tripping on shrooms with people, the whole thing might end with a whisper and not the bang we sought if the local police caught the chatter and got suspicious. Whatever misgivings I might have had, it didn't look like she was going away. She'd cosied up beside me and offered me a few sips from her can of cider. I decided there was only one thing to do from an operational standpoint: I had to read her into the operation, but I had to make sure she was isolated until zero hour. In other words, I had to make sure she had plans for the night.

We wandered up the beach for a while, I told her my story, or rather, I told her Spanx's story, he'd started in Latin American Studies at uni but quit after a year. Since then, he went back home to Coventry for a few months, tried to get a few community projects on the go, but it wasn't what he was looking for. He decided he'd do some travelling. That's how Nicaragua happened, as much by accident as anything. Spanx was in Mexico doing some house building but then he heard about the stuff that went down in Nicaragua in the 1980s, like in that song by The Clash, "Washington Bullets", ("Yeah, I've heard of The Clash, M.I.A. sampled them, didn't she?"). Spanx thought he'd see if he could do anything. It was an eye opener, learned a lot, but somehow it just felt like it was time to come

home. That more or less brought things to now.
"So what's now?"
"Well, the squat, and walking up the beach with a lovely younger lady."
"Where you got her hidden then, Spanx? I wanna meet her."
"There is one other thing though."
"Oh yeah? What is it?"
"Well, I could tell you but I'd have to..."
"Kill me, Spanx? You in MI5 or something like that?"
"On the contrary. I wouldn't have to kill you, but I'd have to know I could trust you."
"Oh, okay so this is more like Cheech and Chong than cloak and dagger is it, Spanx? On the QT?"
"Something like that. Look, let's get away from this shit. I'm tired of running into all these PPE-ple. You know where the whale is?"
"Yeah, Spanx, I kinda have eyes you know."
"Well, there's a quiet place just beyond where he's beached, I'll tell you the tale there."
"How do you know he's a he, eh, Spanx?"

When I told her the plan she laughed at me. That's what I wanted, because it put me in a position where I had to prove myself.
"You think I'm kidding?"
"I think everybody's kidding."
"Then can I show you something?"
"This is how girls get in trouble, Spanx."
"It's cool. Look, how about this."
I gave her the can of pepper spray I kept inside the pocket of the waistcoat I was wearing.
"Insurance, okay?"
"Damn, Spanx, you're prepared. I'm starting to believe you."
I walked with her through the town. It was dark and almost quiet. The moon was full and bright and with the street lamps in the centre of town it was so bright you could almost have forgotten it was night. I took her to where the flatbed was parked. She gave a quick laugh when she saw it. I pressed the

door lock on the key fob and she saw it was mine. She saw I was serious. She stopped laughing.
"Holy shit, Spanx, you're like beyond MI5."
"Yeah, well, nobody's perfect. Look, Psyche, I shouldn't have showed this to you, but I felt like you'd understand."
"I do understand, Spanx. Well, sort of, I mean, this *is* fucking weird."
"It is, but I need you to promise not to tell anyone."
"I was a Brownie once."

I told her what we were planning to do in the morning.
"That's literally amazing, Spanx. You really think you're going to be able to pull that off?"
"I know we will."
"What about the feds?"
"The police? They won't be a problem."
"That's not usually my experience."
I told her about Professor Jonas.
"You could say we're actually working with the police."
"Mr. Spanx, you are one crazy fuck. I love it. Where do I sign up?"

I sent texts to everyone to meet at the flatbed at 0500. I read Blackbird's text from earlier. We were a fair distance from the B&B he'd booked us. I asked Psyche if she wanted to walk there with me.
"That would be sick, Spanx, I need a hosedown. If you don't mind that is."

Dawn spread over Fistral Beach from a silver streak on the horizon. All of us stood together on a cliff overlooking the sea and watched the first patches of pink, and peach and powder blue spread out over against the sea. Looking out over the beach you would have seen people stretched everywhere, on blankets, lovers holding each other, some unfortunates face down and stripped, left to be summoned to their hangovers by the encroaching surf. There was the whale, as stolid and dark as ever, a shipwrecked mountain of irreducible reality darkening

the edges of all our various dreams. I held Psyche's hand as I told everyone to huddle up.
"Nice tie, Spanx," Tomrade said, "all 'House of Windsor' and shit."
"Okay, this is it. We've got a whale to move. We'll need to split up. I'm going down to meet with Officer Friendly over there. Lilith, you, Tomrade, Psyche and the guys get back to the campsite. I'll text when we're ready to move. You're flying point to London, police roadblocks complications of any kind, you tell us. Sneaky Pete, Sneaky Gavin you're coming with me. Nice ties, too, I might add."
"All thanks to you, Spanx. Where'd you find a tie shop this early?"
"I've got my ways," or rather, the owner of the B&B had a drawer full of ties and shirts and other kinds of costumes (police, fire, meter reader, postman, emergency services) in his basement. After Psyche went to sleep I went down and had a rummage.
"All yours captain, just send 'em back washed's all I ask, don't want to put the little lady through anymore than's necessary."
"You two are my lab crew," I said, pointing to the Sneakies, "You just follow my lead, and don't offer anything, but if Officer Friendly or any of his relatives get chatty, lots of tell-you-but-I'd-have-to-kill-you. They press, then it's jargon jargon jargon. Jargon them to death. Cool?"
"I could tell you but--"
"Excellent. Tank? You're the behind the wheel. Okay, that's the story. Let's get going."
Psyche put her arms around me.
"I want to stay with you."
"I'll see you when we get back to London. It'll be fine. Trust me."
"I trust you."
"Wicked."
I kissed her and she went off with Lilith who gave me a not-particularly-friendly stare and Tomrade raised his fist in solidarity with the working class whale stevedores.
This was it. Time to go solo.

I made my way down to the beach with Peter and Gavin beside me. I waved to the officer guarding the whale.
"Officer Hayes?"
"Professor?"
"Yes, glad to meet you. This is James. This is John." I'd come up with the names on the spot and was kicking myself, but luckily Gavin introduced himself as "James Beach" and offered his hand. Confusion averted. Everyone shook hands and exchanged uncomfortable, professional smiles.
"You know the full story?"
"The gist."
"We've got a crane coming down here in about an hour. We need
you to keep these people clear. It's a common procedure, increasingly so, unfortunately, but it has risks, we don't want any problems."
"Dropping old Moby Dick on some MP's kid while he's got a skinful isn't going to look too good, no, indeed, professor. Understand completely. Don't worry, we know what we're doing."
"I trust you implicitly, Officer Hayes. I'm just going to have a look at our friend here to see what kind of shape he's in for travel, James, John, you just hang around and do whatever Officer Hayes tells you to do, okay?"
They nodded, and I walked off and pretended to make measurements of the whale and identify particular features of his physiology as Officer Hayes made his sotto voce enquiries about what was really going on to John and James.
"Another day at the office, lads?"
"Away game actually," James said.
"Bit of fresh air, must be nice. Sorry about all the litter on the beach, not usually like this. We'll get 'em cleared out though."
"Glad to hear it."
"This all part of some big project? You testing something? I know they're saying submarines on the news but you can't trust that bloody shite since they stopped passing us bungs 'cause of the Murdoch thing."

"Just a routine study."
"Yeah, course it is. For all I know this bloody thing is a weapon itself. I was watching a documentary on Youtube the other night about the Yanks back in the Cold War. They were training bloody dolphins to fight the Russians. Expect it's come a fair way since then."
"That's really not our area, sir."
"Course it's not."
"They bothering you, Officer Hayes?"
"Of course not Professor, have two of me own, 'bout the same age. Bit more talkative though. Yours are on the quiet side."
"We keep the radio on in the lab."
"Course you do."
Officer Hayes kept us entertained with stories of policing in Newquay until the crane arrived. Five police cars drove with it in convoy as it made its way to the beach. Officer Hayes rallied the troops and got out his loud hailer. "Here we go," he said, "LADIES AND GENTLEMEN, AS YOU CAN SEE, WE HAVE A FEW VISITORS THIS MORNING. NOTHING TO GET ALL TWITCHY ABOUT, BUT PLEASE DISPERSE! COME NO CLOSER THAN 100 METERS. ANYONE VIOLATING THE CORDON WILL BE SUBJECT TO ARREST! ANYONE VIOLATING THE CORDON WILL BE SUBJECT TO IMMEDIATE ARREST!"

The crane groaned down the beach and bleated to a stop beside the whale's tale. The driver got out, shook my hand and told me it was an honour. I was sweating but I was also freezing from the chilly morning air. It was 6.34 and the possibility of an insomniac Professor Jonas waking up early and sneaking a quick peek at his email was turning my stomach into a minefield. Every second that ticked off I waited for the text message that would come down from Blackbird: ABORT YOU FUCKING ABORTION IN SUNGLASSES, BLOODY ABORT!

The crane driver was telling me about how the coaches down at his kid's school were giving it to him about helping them

do some improvements to the playing fields when I felt my phone go. This is it, I thought. This is the end. We're fucked.
"...And the bloke is like 'Yeah, well it's been five years since anything's been done with them clubhouses and it's austerity Britain now, isn't it? Not a chance from the council.' And I told him, I said, 'Look, mate, do I come round to your place of work--"
"Sorry, I have to take this."
"No worries mate. I'll get strapped in and whatnot."
"Traffic," it was Tank's voice, it was like every nerve in my body suddenly was dropped into a swimming pool filled with gin and tonic, "Bloody traffic. Like there's some kind of police operation going on," he said.
"ETA?"
"It's looking like another fifteen minutes."
Fifteen more minutes for the good professor to stumble on his "sent mail" page, notice the unusual query he'd sent to the chief of police in Newquay in the early hours of the morning, to go to the police, to go to the press, to short-circuit the best laid plans of whales and men...
"Okay, fifteen minutes and the flatbed's here people," I shouted trying to appear as though I knew what I was doing, to appear as though everything were ticking over exactly as planned. I got another text message. My heart nearly split in two.
It was from Psyche.
"Miss you Spanx."
It was the first time I'd consciously exhaled since sunrise. Officer Hayes and his men had set up some mobile bollards on the beach and strung police tape between them. The sun was out and bright now. It would be creeping in through the half-drawn blinds of Professor Jonas' bedroom in a few minutes time. He'd be stretching his arms over his head. He'd be wiping his eyes. He'd be leaving the toilet. He'd be setting the kettle on. He'd be switching on his computer right about now. Waiting for it to warm up, to send him his daily greetings...
"Professor?"

It was James.
"What is it?"
"I've got, uh, Mr. Raymond on the line. He wants to know if the pathway is clear."
"Tell him to pull up to the edge of the beach. We're ready."

And we were ready. The crane guy locked the pincer down around the whale's tail, and slowly raised its massive body up. A scene kept playing out in my mind where the whale came crashing to the ground, its tail ripped from its body, the blood spraying over everyone gathered around the police tape. There were hundreds of people now, some of them clapping and cheering, why that was, God only knew, some were swigging cans of Red Stripe and chatting, some were taking images with their smartphones. I saw the whale in my mind slipping from the crane, smashing down on a whole section of this crowd, crushing ten, twenty people, ambulances, more police, headlines screaming. Blackbird screaming. As I watched the theatrical carnage erupt from behind the scrim of my eyes it hit me what was really happening, where the real crisis was. It wasn't the whale falling to earth and squashing an entire year of A-Level students from Nottingham, it was every one of those little smartphone snaps of the whale in the air. They first wave had been taken now. They'd been tweeted, and instagrammed and they'd been put up on Snapchat and faded away in to the ether. By now, there would be people drawing smiley faces on the whale with Photoshop. Cut-and-Pasting the Prime Minister's head onto the whale and turning it into a dancing screensaver. It would be going viral. By the time it was lowered onto the flatbed, there'd be a story on the BBC website, gig posters featuring the whale wearing a gold chain and announcing DJ nights up and down Kingsland Road, and Professor Jonah, God bless him, would be neck-deep in ambergris.

As the whale hung over the flatbed, the beach was in a state of unearthly quiet. Everyone had stopped cheering and shouting and they were watching the crane as it maneuvered the whale into position to drop it into place on the flatbed. The whale swayed in the sea wind as the crane's arm lowered, the head gently touched the edge of the flatbed and the pincer let go. The rest of the whale dropped with a cold thwack onto the bed. The crowd started screaming and hooting again. "Back of the net," I heard someone say. Tank, the Sneakies, and the driver tied the whale down with a tarpaulin and steel cables to keep it from sliding around. I jumped up on the crane shook hands with the driver and then went over to thank Officer Hayes for his cooperation and tell him we'd be on our way.

Just toward the edge of the beach where it met the road I saw them advancing. Television trucks, reporters, fuzzy microphones, cameramen with gear that looked like it came out of some kind of weapons lab. It might as well have, it was all aimed straight at me. It was like a dream. The sand slowed me down as I ran. Officer Hayes saw me coming. I stopped. I pointed to the camera crews. "We tried to hold them off. Told them we had a press conference for 9.30AM in the station," he called, "They must have seen it on bloody Twitter or Instatwat or whatever it's called."
"I'm going to go. Thanks for everything."
"Don't mention it."
"I didn't."
I turned and ran toward the flatbed. The first reporters were skittering down the beach. Officer Hayes and the police moved on them.
"Whoa, gentlemen and ladies, this is a closed area."
"It's not a closed area, there's nothing saying it's a closed area. There weren't any announcements on the web--"
"It's a closed area now."
"Is she secure," I shouted as I pulled open the door of the flatbed cab.
Tank gave me a thumbs up.
"Then let's fucking drive!"

Chapter VI: The Belly of the Beast

On the way into London my brain was critical and nearing meltdown. We'd dropped our number plates outside Bristol but I was still sure there'd be enough on social media to make it child's play in tracking us down. Raymond texted Lilith every fifteen minutes to ensure the roads we were going down were clear of police. I knew we'd be on every CCTV camera on the motorway, every speed camera, but I couldn't risk village traffic, so we just had to push it. Sneaky Gavin thought it might be relaxing to listen to some inane podcast he liked, Lefthanded Cigarettes. We put it on the speakers, some half-stoned DJ taking phone calls: "It really annoys me that I can't decide which is the better joke, calling it the "Hammersmith-Shitty Line" or the "Hammershit and City Line".

"The second one sounds like you're making fun of Hammersmith, mate."

"Yeah, I know, and that's not my intention"

And so on for most of the next three hours.

At Shepherd's Bush there was a massive bottleneck. Then I saw it, police had shut down traffic. This was it. We were done. I saw the police as I'd never seen them before, as an alien force to be resisted, outsmarted and defeated. It was the first time I felt it, really felt it inside me, not inside "Spanx", like I'd crossed over and wasn't acting, like it was really me against my old mates. The plan I had was going to be painful. When they came to us I'd just gun the engine and plow through the roadblock and take their cars with me. There was enough power in Mad Mick's flatbed to get us past them, but then they'd be looking for us. I texted Blackbird to let him know we'd "beached", our code word for arriving in London. It was a thousand years before he replied though we'd moved two inches.

"Glad you're here. Don't worry about the Good Shepherds its just a traffic light."

And, looking up, it was just a traffic light. The police were everywhere but they didn't seem to be doing anything. There were just a few guys in the intersection waving people through and halting them. It took another twenty minutes but they waved us on without so much as a glance. All the way to

Battersea it felt like we were flying.

I couldn't believe what I was seeing when I got to the power station. I'd expected to find it in its usual state of stolid disrepair and silence, but it was almost as insane as the beach we'd left that morning. I stopped the flatbed in the car park. Lilith ran up to meet me.
"We thought, there's no point in keeping this a secret."
"You went rogue in other words."
"Have you seen social media?"
"No, actually, I've been transporting a stolen whale carcass across the West Country so I've been too busy to check my Twitter account."
She handed me her smart phone, "well, we have."
Stories were everywhere. The BBC was reporting that "questions were emerging about the removal of a whale from a beach in Newquay this morning."

If you believed the story:

> *A group of men purporting to be from the government office, CEFAS, including one claiming to be Professor Jonah Higgins removed the body of the whale at approximately 7AM GMT using heavy equiment and a large transport lorry. When reporters attempted to reach Professor Higgins at CEFAS, they were told he did not report to work and that the office knew nothing of an operation to remove the whale for study. Later it emerged that Professor Higgins had been in police custody during the day.*
>
> *Since the incident, video and images of the whale's removal have been circulating on social media, all show a very sophisticated operation to get the whale off the beach. It can be seen being lifted by a crane and lowered onto a flatbed lorry. A number of websites and Twitter postings have suggested the operation may have been a complicated heist postulating involvement of groups including organised criminal syndicates trafficking in whale blubber, ambergris,*

and whale ivory to environmental extremists. The offices of CEFAS have not issued a public statement at the time this story went to press.

"Then it's out there."
"So are you."
She showed me the Twitter feed of a journalist for the Guardian, Toby Montreaux. He'd posted someone's video of me speaking to Officer Hayes. He'd written:
"Doesn't look like Professor Higgins to me. #whaletheft."
"They're everywhere," Lillith said.
She was right. Hashtags like "#grandtheftorca" and "#whalenapper" were trending. We had to get ahead of the story if only to keep any actual activists from sending Operation AHAB out the blow-hole. I decided to write to Toby Montreaux.
After a call to Blackbird, I had Toby Montreaux's personal email.
"Been watching that gnome-fucker for months now. Never bloody does anything remotely worthwhile like, just fucking gnomes in Leicestershire car parks like a good little gnome-fucker. All he does is watch classical music videos on Youtube to pass the time between mail-order gnomes. We've got someone working on making things more interesting. Trust me."

Dear Toby,

You've written some awfully naughty tweets about me. You should be careful who you stigmatise, not everyone is as philosophical about being patronised by middle-aged white men as my friends and I. As you can imagine, my professional life as a marine biologist in the service of HMG has many discontents and sometimes I find I need to get away to somewhere quiet where I can get in touch with nature, a place like Newquay.

I wanted you to know our cousin the whale is in a safe place. He'll be contributing to a cause larger than military science. We wanted to keep things secret until a time of our choosing, but the we decided it was necessary to stop the rumours about the incident in Newquay having something to do with trafficking. That's something we could never condone or encourage. Retweet after us: Whales are not commodities!

It's fitting that after having been murdered by our endless blind pursuit of militarism that his legacy will ultimately be as an icon of social and environmental justice. Toby, I know nature is close to your heart, even if you live in Stoke Newington, 16B Cazenove Road, N16, and I promise you that when you see our cousin again, he'll make you proud. I only ask that you stand with us in our cause, the cause of exposing the criminal activities of our government in our name.

Yours in solidarity,
Professor Jonah Higgins

It sounds deluded now, but at the time, I felt like it was something of a masterstroke asking Toby Montreaux to "support" us. I knew he'd be too arrogant to keep the email a secret and when it came out, the fact that we asked him for "support" in "our" cause would give Blackbird and Company a little to work with in their own investigation of him. It would also mean one of two things, either he would actively support us, both implicating himself in our crimes and discrediting him in the wider public, or he would refuse and denounce us and thus lose influence in the environmental community. I wasn't particularly surprised when about two minutes after I'd sent him the email, I got a message back asking if I minded if he made the letter public.
"I think people need to know what happened and why. I'll redact your email of course, and my home address, thank you very much. If the police come around the offices you can count on me to stand by you."
"We're worried about the police," I wrote back, "how can we know we can trust you?"

"You don't know. I'm sure you've taken precautions though. I can actually offer you some advice, I'm sure you're on the TOR network. They can't break into that. You should use cheap mobiles, too. I'm probably only telling you things you already know."

Or things you've watched on The Wire.

"We'll send you a message before the reveal. Just don't try to find us."

"I can respect that. And thank you."

I could almost read the story of his heroic reporting and confidential sources "close to an environmental movement which appears to have been behind the removal of the whale from Fistral Beach in Newquay (some would use the word "theft" here, but how can one steal part of nature? It offends common sense like the purchase of human flesh)."

I went back to the power station. There was a silent rave happening. I looked around and saw people dancing with each other but there was no music. Then I saw that they were all using ipods and had their own playlists. Tank saw me and hurried over.

"We told them no music. They improvised."

"We'll move to phase two tomorrow morning at dawn."

"Phase two?"

"The hanging."

As I said this, I saw Psyche moving out from the crowd. I watched her smile gathering in her face as she saw me, that perfect row of teeth, those slightly sleepy brown eyes narrowing a bit, her hair was twisted over her head in a long braid now. She started to jog toward me and threw her arms around my neck. She took a step back then pulled my head down for a kiss.

"They wouldn't tell me anything about you. I didn't know if I'd see you again or if it was all some kind of game where you just sort of gave me to your friends to get rid of me. I just can't believe all of this. Or any of it! It's amazing!"

"Don't believe it. Don't believe any of it, it'll be better for you."

"You have to show me the whale. Where is it?"
"Come on."
She took my hand and we walked out toward the flatbed. I undid some of the hooks around where the whale's head was resting and lifted up the tarpaulin.
"It looks so peaceful."

I left Psyche to talk to my crew about hanging the whale in the morning. I was giving directions to the Sneakies but my mind was with her, passing back into the crowd, following the back of her head until she disappeared. I snapped out of it. I told them I wanted to get the whale up quickly so that it dominated the day's headlines, maybe even attracted a crowd at lunch time so there could be maximum confusion and opportunity to scoop people up. We talked through logistics and Tank suggested that we gut the whale to make sure that if it did fall it wouldn't do as much damage. We decided that we'd present the gutting as a ritual, something participatory so that people would both keep busy and stay on site and so that, when the time came, more people would, literally, have blood on their hands.

Tank hooked up a little PA system in the main room of the station and I stood in the middle of the crowd.
"People, thank you all for coming. This means a lot. Everyone applauded. Psyche appeared from the crowd to stand in the front trying to find my eyes. I motioned for quiet and began again.
"We're part of something historic tonight. Everyone here is making a very clear statement about the kind of world they want to live in. I couldn't be prouder to see so many people from so many backgrounds here, but I want you to know, our job doesn't end here. What we've done so far, liberated the whale, given our friends and fans in the police departments a bit of a headache, that's just step one. I want to tell you that we've got a plan. A plan to make our whale the last victim of militarism and ecocidal violence. But I need your help, because the next step is complicated. So, I know a lot of you are vegetarian-vegan and fishing isn't your kind of thing, but everyone else who's been fishing knows, if you catch it, you've got to clean

it. What we need right now is some people to volunteer to help me clean up our friend the whale because he's got a big day ahead of him tomorrow and I want him to look nice. Can I see some hands from people who want to help out?"

A forest of hands shot up, the applause was deafening. Even the PA couldn't make me audible, I just pointed toward the door and everyone followed me out. It only took about 90 minutes to get the whale cleaned. Some of the viscera we left in a corner for compost, but some people insisted on using some of the organs for food. I told them it wasn't my call, it wasn't my whale. When I ran into them an hour later they were making whale haggis in the one of the kitchens in the plant.
"We're going to take it out to the men's shelter in the morning."
"That's beautiful," I said.
That night, Psyche and I went for a walk around the grounds of the powerstation. Most people were asleep except for a few guys juggling sticks in the dark.
"I really didn't expect my weekend to end up this way."
"I'm just glad you're here to witness it."
"I still don't understand how you guys got in here, this place must be overrun with security."
"There was, uh, there was a 'changing of the guards' type thing. It's normally guarded by the feds but they're switching over to a private company. We got in before they did. Sneaky-sneaky, you know?"
"You guys are amazing. You're like fucking superheroes or something."
The moonlight was clear and white along the waste ground around Battersea powerstation. It was so quiet you could hear the Thames washing up just beyond the bridge. It looked for all the world like a beach and somehow nothing could have been more natural at that moment than the giant, silent frame of the whale sleeping in the shadow of the towers.
"I know this is crazy," she said, "but I want to see inside of it."
"It's a bit mucky in there still. We cleaned it, but..."
"I don't care."
She climbed up onto the flatbed and pulled me up

beside her. She pulled back a flap of the whale's skin and peered inside at the massive archways of its skeleton. "It's so delicate. It's beautiful, like a cathedral or something."
I was creeped out by the whole thing. When I signed up for Operation CHSTERTON I hadn't expected it would entail squatting between the ribs of a gutted whale, but there I was, Psyche beside me. You could hear the muted city outside, the flap of skin closed over us and shut out the light. Psyche pulled me close and kissed me. I hesitated for a moment.
"No, I want to, it'll be okay," she said. I wasn't sure what she wanted to do, or what would be okay; in fact, I was pretty sure the opposite was true, still though, I let her move on top of me and unbutton my shirt. She kissed me, took her top off and said, "Pretend we're back on the beach." I'd become very good at pretending.

Chatper VII: Whalerise

In the morning, after I sent Tank to pick up a crane, I emailed Toby Montreaux.
"Midday: Battersea Powerstation. Whalerise."
He didn't reply, but I knew he'd be there. I was nervous but everything seemed to be going to plan, which was mad enough on its own. I'd texted Blackbird first thing in the morning and told him the details. He couldn't have been happier. Peter and Gavin had been feeding him information all day, he had more mobile numbers than he knew what to do with.
"Sure, we've got the mobile numbers already, that's just trapdoors, though, now we've got names and we can build up profiles. The orcs are loving it. The floor's ankle deep in orc spunk, it's a beautiful sight, but bring a change of socks when you're back in the office. Beats the everloving shit out of those bloody Marxist reading groups we spent years setting up."

Out on the grounds people had started to wake up and a crowd was gathered. The usual jugglers and hacky-sack players were in their little circles. People were sipping coffee. From time to time I'd see Sneaky Pete or Sneaky Gavin surface and give me a nod. Lilith was monitoring social media inside and Tank was still on the road. It was almost symphonic. Then I felt a sharp blow on my back. I was on auto-pilot, I grabbed the arm instinctively flung my attacker to the ground only to discover it was Tomrade. I took my knee off his head and let him catch his breath.
"Fuck, bro, they teach you that shit in Nicaragua? Or Vauxhall?"
"Sorry, mate, I got carried away, I'm so fucking nervy. Got anything to chase the hungry ghosts away?"
Tomrade produced a bag of skunk and he rolled me a joint. He was still a little wary, I could tell. Though I wasn't planning to inhale, you can never really resist strong skunk and you find yourself half-stoned just being in the same postcode as a couple of smokers. I thought I'd try to get as much of an explanation as I could together before the paranoia set in.
"Sorry again about jacking you back there. Nerves. I was

a third level master in *capoeira*, sometimes it comes out. I learned it at a coffee plantation I was working on in Brazil back before Nicaragua."

"Thought you were in Mexico before Nic, bro."

"I was, but I was in Brazil before I went there. Gap year and that kind of Lavabit."

Though it was always difficult to tell with Tomrade, he'd clearly loosened up and smiled. I think he was flattered I'd finally picked up the 99% slang.

"*Capoeira* Jedi," he said, then he began to chuckle his low-pitched fag-scarred chuckle, "Got to teach me some of that shit, Spanx. Kung fu fighting, yeah? Have to agree, it was a little bit frightening."

"Soon as we get orca up I'll show you some throws." As I said this I heard the squeak of a horn. It was the crane. Tank was here. It was Whalerise.

It was an incredible sight. The crane hoisting the whale, the cheers, the shouts, the chanting. Tank maneouvered the whale between the two smokestacks at the front of the station. A few people had volunteered to spot on the roof. The Sneakies were there to oversee the anchoring of the whale to the towers. It was all surprisingly delicate, watching the whale ascend into the cloudy summer sky, floating there like an apparition then moving in a strange horizontal way like something from a video game. It sounds mad now, but it was a kind of magic. Psyche was beside me her arms tight round my waist, her head resting on my shoulder. There was a profound feeling of community among everyone there. We were all willing the whale into place on the rooftop. Just a few more inches this way, just a bit that way, come on boys, I head cars arriving, I knew it was the media. Toby Montreaux had come through. Using thick steel cables wrapped in leather the spotters secured the whale's tale, and then, with everyone in the crowd holding their breath, they started pushing the whale forward until it slipped off the roof and the cables caught it. Success! For a moment it felt like all the oxygen in the world had been sucked away and then the roar of the crowd went up. Whalerise!

The whole crowd went silent and we just watched him hang there. The only sound was the clicking of cameras and the noise of trains and the river in the distance. I heard some voices drawling out in South London patois. I turned round. It was a group of fifteen year olds in baseball caps digging into a big box of Stella.

"Fuckin' Moby Dickhead, innit, blud?"

Then, it could only have been a few minutes later but it felt like another century, I heard the wail of police sirens. Phase two. They, or possibly I should say 'we', came in faster than I thought. Suddenly we were all surrounded. Police in riot gear charged toward us with batons out. The crowd didn't know what was happening at first but somewhere off to one side of the mass a struggle started and soon we were inside a hurricane of flailing batons and riot shields. Everything that had seemed so peaceful and harmonious the moment before was suddenly blown every which way. I was frozen. I couldn't even blink as I watched the police running everywhere people throwing juggling sticks and whale viscera at them, some special teams were already out rappelling down the side of the power station to cut the whale free. The cameras were frantic now. Reporters and photographers slamming into police, slamming into activists, slamming into the ground. I reached to pull Psyche closer to me but she was gone. I called out even though I knew she couldn't hear me. I kept screaming her name when I heard a sound so powerful I thought the police had brought some kind of cannon with them. But it wasn't a cannon, it was the whale smashing to the earth into a pile of ripped skin and bones. "Psyche..." I called, but there was no answer.

Chapter VIII: Post-Mortem

By the end of the day they'd taken nearly everyone into custody. They'd set up a kettle around the entire building and pressed us in. I heard that it took them, us, hours to make all the arrests. I was arrested with a group of other people and we were sat in the back of a wagon packed tight for about half an hour before anything happened. We saw shadows moving outside the window. Someone came into the wagon and pointed to me.

"That's the ratfucker in question."

Another policeman said, "Come with us, nature boy."

They grabbed me by the neck and forced me out of the van. One officer gave me a kick in the arse once I was on the ground.

"Just testing it out for later, mate. You're going to have a whale of a time in prison."

I heard someone call out "We're witnesses, Spanx," as they hauled me away.

"Witnesses? Even if Jehovah witnessed it you lot aren't getting off," he said staring them down.

"Where are you taking me?"

"Very inquisitive all of a sudden aren't we, Nature Boy?"

He threw me to the ground.

"Whoops. I'm gettin' clumsy in me old age. Let me help you."

He gave me a couple of smacks with the baton in the ribs and then he pulled me up.

"Now, then, must be more careful. Don't want that to happen again, do we? It's just that I get so distracted when people talk to me, it makes me do things I regret later. Whoops!"

He threw me down and booted me in the face. Then he brought the baton down on the back of my head when I reached for my face.

"Okay, sorry about that mate, you know how it is. When I get talking I just don't know where me head's at. But it's alright. You're in good hands with me. I've got some mates on the force — some wrong 'uns that lot. Almost as bad as you, but we make 'em shower more often. Now, got any more questions, before we get walking again mate? I don't want to get distracted again. Walkin' and talkin' ain't in me contract, see. Police union, innit. It's a high risk job, don't want to do

meself an injury. Or anyone else for that matter."
I didn't say anything. He brought me to a parked car around the back of the station. The windows were blacked out. For a minute I felt the fear. Standing there seeing my blood stained face in the reflection of the glass. It could only have been Blackbird, of course waiting for me in the car. When he opened the door he looked at Mr. Clumsy.
"Clumsy fucker."
"It'll be the death of me, sir."
"Just might, Tommy fucking Cooper," he said, tossing me against the bonnet of his car, "Smell Gibson here's my problem now. I'd advise you to return to your ballet lesson, you graceful little bum bandit."
The officer turned away and Blackbird threw me into the passenger seat of his car.
"Felt like you'd enjoy the authentic tourist experience," he said when he sat beside me.
"Good day?"
"Very good day. All sorts of maggots squirming around on that carcass. Couldn't be happier. You lot will need a bit of a holiday while the cameras are flashing. I hope you're not planning on selling your story to OK or anything in the next week, Spanx, that's your name now, right?"
"Not now."
"Yes, now and until we're finished with this. This is just bloody chapter one, Spanxy Boy."
"What next?"
"Well, we wait and see what kind of vermin start scurrying now that we've turned the tiki torches on. Also, you're in big trouble, some saddlebag calling himself Mad Mick reported you to us for stealing his flatbed. Naughty, naughty dickhead."

Chapter IX: Exile

I'd never been to Dove Cottage. I'd never even heard of it, and I certainly didn't expect to find myself there immediately after Whalerise, but when they let me out of the blacked out van, there I was, standing outside Wordsworth's old house in the Lake District as if it were the most logical thing in the world.

"This is the place?" I asked.

"It is, sir. Said to be very restful."

"What about the tourists?"

"Tourists, sir?"

"The people who come to the cottage."

"That's all been taken care of, sir."

"Taken care of?"

"Cover sir. The head of RBS rented it out for a holiday as far as the literary world is concerned. Something else for them to write angry letters about, sir. Those of them who can read, that is."

He led me up to the door of the cottage and Blackbird was inside.

"Welcome home."

"Thank you, sir."

"You took his phone?"

"Yes, sir," the driver said.

"Yeah, well, we're gonna do a little more thorough search upstairs in a minute, that okay with you, Spanx?"

"Fine sir."

"Thought so. Kind of thing that's right up your street, or your back passage as it were."

"You're here for a month. We'll bring you everything you need. You don't read the newspaper, you don't check your email, you don't update your status because you don't have any status, you're ghosts. You're in 'solitary confinement' until we get properly ahead of the story. Until then, sit here. You read these things," he picked up some books from a shelf and dropped them on the floor, "they're old enough to be safe. Blokey McBloke here'll drop by in the mornings to make sure you're not throwing your shit at each other, unless that's the sort of thing you've gotten into since life with the comrades. Or the Tomrades."

We both smiled. “He’s got a real spirit that bleeder. Banging on about his bloody human rights all the time he was. You know how that goes, ‘bang, bang bang’.”
His smile disappeared and he told “Blokey” he could leave.
“Right, sir,” he said.
When he left us alone Blackbird rolled his eyes and said, “Lovely little gestapo that lad. He’s even got me worried. He starts growing a moustache we’re all in trouble. Thing is, Spanx, I like that name for you. Should change it by deed poll when all this is said and done, thing is, much as I hate to admit it, you done good as they say in the cop shows.”
“Thank you, sir.”
“Don’t thank me,” he said, “thank yourself,” he made a the universal ‘wanker’ motion with his hand, “This next month is going to be serious shit. The media hounds are out and there’ve been some unexpected complications.”
“Complications, sir?”
“Yeah, nothing that you need to trouble your smelly little dreadlocks about, just a bit of logistical difficulties. We’ll be able to land the plane okay. What I need you to do though is to keep the animals quiet until we do. That means none of you leave the grounds. You’ve got fair bit of freedom here. You can take walks, got the bloody sky, the bloody hills, the bloody fucking lake, all that rubbish but nobody goes near a fucking communication device. Blokey can’t be here 24-7 so you’re my eyes and ears the rest of the time. I’m trusting you and that’s why I’m giving you this.”
He pulled a 9mm from his pocket and handed it to me.
“Sir, I don’t think…”
“I’m telling you, Spanky, if anything happens, if any unexpected noises come from backstage, I’ve got another one of these things,” he pulled it out, “and I have to tell you there are a lot of plausible stories about what could ‘happen’ to you. Its not just about us anymore.”
“Who is it about?”
“That’s the kind of shit you have 28 days to learn to stop giving a shit about. I’ll be here at the weekends. Need to catch up on my fishing. In the meantime, relax, boyo. You’ve earned

it."
Blackbird waved with the gun in his hand and then got into his car. I went inside the house and two officers met me.
"Upstairs, please."
They grabbed my arms and hustled me through the cottage to a toilet and they stripped me down.
They were completely confident I had no communication devices on, or in, my person when they were through with me. When they left I thought I was alone, but then I saw Raymond and Martha in the garden drinking tea. For a moment I thought it was a hallucination.
"Here he is, General Spanx."
"I'm fucking glad to see the two of you."
"Peter and Gav are out on the lake. Rowing."
"So I was the last one."
"You were. I think they trust you least, Spanx. You're too good," Raymond said.
"I could do for a cuppa."
"You'll have to make your own," Martha said. She held up the teapot and Raymond brought it to me.
"I'll help you out. You look suitably helpless."
We went inside and got some water on the boil.
"They took your phone too," I asked.
"Dignity too, my friend, my dignity too..."
"Oh well, a chance to get away from it alright."
"What did he tell you?"
"What about?"
"What about..."
"He gave you the same talk?"
"The operational glitches."
"Something like that."
"You find out what it means?"
"Not really my concern."
Raymond poked around a bit more, but I cut him off at every turn. The last thing I needed was someone adding to the questions I was storing up myself. Not that there were very many in the beginning, I was still "high" from the success of Operation AHAB. I have to say that for a moment I did

feel like the captain of a very powerful ship. I was taking the department into new territory, boldly going where no one had dared to dream of going before. Police work always has a creative dimension, trying to piece together some set of events from the evidence you're left with, trying to make a connection between people and places that you know is there, but just can't quite reach. This project was somewhere between being a rock and roll star and James Bond. I was happy, I won't deny it. What would I have had to be unhappy about? I was a rising star and everywhere I looked I was surrounded by beauty. I treated those first days like a spa weekend, waking up around 11AM and going for walks by the lakes. Staring out into the layered greens of the hills and water, the grey waves of clouds that you could almost reach out and touch, wild flowers, the little cottages and the grass. I knew we couldn't go beyond a certain radius or a tag around my ankle would go off, but there was enough on the grounds to keep me busy. I read Wordsworth's writings. I'd never bothered with them at school, all of it seemed a bit poncy to me, but sitting there in his house, it all made sense. It was only after the first month that there started to be issues.

Blackbird had told us that we were expected to be called back to duty after four weeks but on the Sunday of the fourth week, Blackbird came up for his usual debrief and told us that there'd been some complications.
"Look, it's one of these interagency things. Six villages fighting over the same goat or whale or whatever you want. You guys are only my secret weapon if you stay a secret, right? Right. So, give me another week and I'll bring you back to civilisation. In the meantime, here's some reading material."
Blackbird left us with some research on hydraulic fracturing. He said our next mission should centre on energy production, possibly even targetting specific companies.
I have to admit, I think we were all going a bit stir crazy by this point. Raymond in particular was desperate to get back to civilisation.
"I've devolved. I'm now somebody's cottage negro."
We all sat around one evening trying to figure out what it was

that was keeping us locked up.
"I hate to tell you this, guys, but I think it's me. I think it's something I did," Martha said.
She told me about the night before Newquay how she'd been working on a guy in Brixton, "Pinky", who ran a Rastafarian shop and claimed he was an albino.
"You know how it is, we have to live the life, right? Well, we were back at his place and things were getting a little bit cozy and he tells me he wants to film it. Well, I told him it was a dealbreaker, but he had the tripod all set up. If he'd switched it on somehow...it would only have taken a second...I made a note to check it in the morning, but things got going so fast there wasn't time."
"You're telling me there's a sex video of you?"
"I'm not saying there is a sex video of me, I'm saying there might be a sex video of me." (Note to the reader, yes, unfortunately there was a video, www.eyeporn.com/grendls_milf_swallows_beowulfs_sword/anglo_suction_myth. That is, there was until The Sneakies did a little bit of hacking.)
"Presumably one where you and Rastaman fuck each other with Grendel's arm for a dildo."
"Look, you fucking--"
Peter grabbed Martha and Gavin made to grab me. Raymond pulled me down from behind.
"Look, this is accomplishing nothing," he said, "if this is anybody's fault it's yours, Mr. Spanx,"
"Fuck off, Raymond."
"Hey, I'm only being real, right? Okay, so we're out here in WickerMan country, there's nothing we can do, we might as well try to get along before we all go cannibal on each other."
Martha was sitting on Dorothea Wordsworth's writing desk and I was against the opposite wall with Gavin about an inch from my face.
"Now let's all kiss and make up and try to make the best of this shit. You think it's easy for a black guy to be up here? Anybody sees me and they'll probably order a drone strike on this place." Raymond insisted that we all eat dinner together that night.

"We need to rebuild the spirit we had back at the squat. It was okay then, wasn't it," I asked.
"Okay-ish, you lot listen to The Killers too damn much," Raymond said.
Everyone was in the kitchen busy with various tasks, Peter chopping leeks, Martha at the stove frying onions. Raymond was mashing potatoes and Gavin was stirring herbs into some of the organic ground beef that the last supply drop left us with. We made shepherd's pie and drank a few bottles of wine. Peter suggested we all read some of Wordsworth's poetry out loud.
"Maybe" he said, "it would do us some good."
We passed around the collected works and selected a poem each. Peter read "Tintern Abbey". When he came to the bit where the poem reads, "Nature never did betray/ The heart that loved her" and ends up with the bit about how;

> she can so inform
> The mind that is within us, so impress
> With quietness and beauty, and so feed
> With lofty thoughts, that neither evil tongues,
> Rash judgements nor the sneers of selfish men,
> Nor greetings where no kindness is, nor all
> The dreary intercourse of daily life,
> Shall e'er prevail against us, or disturb
> Our cheerful fate.

I heard his voice crack a little bit. He caught himself, but we'd all heard it and he smiled a bit embarrassed but we all laughed and the evening just sort of took off from there. I read "The World is Too Much With Us". Raymond read "To Toussaint L'Ouverture" which I gather was about some Haitian revolutionary. Raymond knew the whole story. What really caught me about that one was the line about the guy's head being "Pillowed in some deep dungeon's earless den". Of course it made me think of our situation, shut off from everything alone in the world--when Martha read "I Wandered Lonely as a Cloud" I think we all knew what he was talking about. It was the first time since we'd been shut up that I actually wondered what had become of everyone who'd been there at Whalerise. Where was Tomrade now? Where was The Dove Row Tag Crew? What was Pinky doing now? And Psyche?

When we finished reading, everyone was exhausted. I think the rest of the team got their first good night's sleep since the first week we'd been up there. For me though, I found it hard. I don't know the right word here, it wasn't exactly a sense that what we were doing was wrong, but that there might be consequences that we hadn't fully understood when we started, consequences that maybe weren't exactly what we'd intended. The world didn't seem as black and white as even a few hours before.

The next day, we did the same thing, dinner, Wordsworth, a bottle of wine.

"I'm glad we're all on speaking terms again. Whatever is happening out there, we have to stick together, we need to be on each other's sides. And to make that easier, we need to communicate. I've been thinking about this for a few days, and I think it's important that we're open with each other. I think we should have a meeting after dinner every night where we just talk things through, if something is bothering someone, we need to hear it, and we need to work through it. We need to share our feelings."

"Is this you or Spanx talking," Raymond asked.

"It's both of us. I'm starting to think there were some things Spanx did and said that weren't as crazy as they seemed at the time."

Peter raised his hand.

"I've been thinking, I mean, I've always kind of felt the same thing. Maybe we can learn something, like something real, from the people we were. It might even make us better police."

"I wouldn't count on that," Raymond said.

"So it's agreed, we meet up every night? We talk this through? We get through this as a team?"

Everyone raised their hands. I felt proud not just of myself, but of the group, that we were capable of seeing the bigger picture. We agreed we'd meet up and we'd read a poem to start the session and then we'd pass the book around, whoever had the book could speak and no one could interrupt until they had the book. When I told the group this, Raymond stood up and started checking the books on the shelf.

"What are you doing?"

"Making sure there isn't a copy of *Lord of the Flies* here."

I understood his skepticism but we had no choice.

At the weekend meeting Blackbird told us a bit about the problem.

"So, I can't lie to you, well, I can't keep lying to you. First, there's a kerfuffle related to the bloody whale thing, apparently, and somebody forgot to look this one up, whales are considered royal fishes, and so they're actually property of Her Majesty. Now, you'd think that would be good news, but since we're deep cover, technically we can't own up, at least not yet. There could be other legal complications, there's actually an operation out there looking for you lot. Well, actually just you Spanxy boy and Jack and Jill Off over there, " he said pointing to Peter and Gavin, "They've got you on tape. The thing is it's not the sort of thing we can just laugh off as a little misunderstanding between friends. Even if we blew the operation you'd still be dick-and-or-cunt deep in whaleshit. Also, there's a small matter of Dr. Jonah. The old piss puddle's decided to be a man of principle about the whole arrest thing. We've got some people looking after his computer at the moment so that he shuts up sooner rather than later, but it's taking more time fixing those bloody time stamp things than we'd like and so he's not quite out of the picture yet. In the meantime, I need you to hang tight. We'll spring you out soon."

After dinner that night, and after reading "Michael" from the *Lyrical Ballads*, Gavin asked for the book. He stood in the middle of the circle, cleared his throat and said something that

changed our lives.
“I don’t quite know how to say this. You see, like all of us, I’ve had a lot of time to, well, for lack of a better word, to think about what we’ve been doing, what we are doing, and what will happen when they send us back. I’m starting to think that maybe I don’t want to be involved when we go back. I think I may have to leave the force.”
Pete stood up, asked for the book and Gavin handed it to him.
“I feel the same way. When Blackbird was here today, I could barely listen to a word he was saying it was like hearing a pneumatic drill ripping up a pavement smacking and jangling up your nerves every which way. I think I’m out when we go back too.”
Raymond looked over at me to see what I was making of all of it. My face was impassive. There was something building inside me too, and before I knew what I was doing, I was reaching out my hand and accepting the book from Gavin. “I had the same feeling,” I said. “When I sleep, I see the whale being hoisted up between those towers, all those people below, the hope they felt. I feel like a traitor, but I’m not sure what to. Maybe I’ve been a traitor all my life and I’m just now discovering what it means to be loyal.”
Raymond came over and asked for the book.
“Tell you all a little story,” he said, “about how our esteemed colleagues conducted themselves when they threw me in the van. One guy in particular. Cuffed down and got right up in my face and said, ‘Just like fuckin’ Gori Island isn’t it, mate?’ So I thought, ‘I’m going to fucking kill this guy and enjoy it, Blackbird’ll sort out his funeral on the QT, but then something stopped me. I said to myself, if I fuck this guy up, if I rip out his intestines and saw his rib cage into bite-sized little pieces, then it’s not me that’s going down, it’s those kids from the power station. What I do becomes part of their story, and I couldn’t do it. So I sat there and the bloke starts in on this disquisition on race and history, cause he understands all of it, of course, “We’re all Africans, mate, when it all started at least. I know that much…” And then it becomes some kind

of fucked up motivational speech, 'In Africa you were kings, rulers of the roost back home, so to speak, and then us lot came over there and then you were slaves. It's not pretty a pretty bit o' watercolour, that I'll agree to, but you were in a primitive state then compared to us. It's just the facts. And I know the facts, mate, read all about it. Youtube, too. I know all that pisses you lot off and, God's truth, I think you maybe have a point sometimes, but you live in our society, you have to play by our rules, simple as that. That's all we're asking. I mean, I like your lot, really, it's true. Mate of mine's black. Good footballer, respect, you know. But not all white people are like me. Not everyone on this force gets you people the way I do. Like I said, you have to play the game innit? Trim and shave, put on a shirt with a collar, get down the job centre and make something of yourself. You need to get an education, you need to pull your socks up. You can't be a fucking nigger all your life you know? You need to respect yourself or nobody else is going to respect you.' And that's just the shit I remember. I had that little speech in my mind all the way up here and I've had it in there ever since, and I think to myself, this guy is on my side? This guy is doing *my* job? This is what *I'm* protecting? This is what *I'm* part of playing for Captain Spanx and his Wanx? No, not for me. Not anymore."

Martha took the book next.

"So it seems like we've all been thinking the same thing, but has it occurred to you that the choice may not be ours anymore?"

Martha was voicing the fear that I think we were all contemplating in the back of our heads: whatever we might want to do, we weren't going to be allowed to do it.

"I for one don't care. I can't take what we're doing anymore," I said, "we have to turn whatever they may have in store for us into our own plan."

"Good luck on that," Raymond said.

The following week when Blackbird came, he told us that we were clear to leave. He also gave us our new assignment. We were to set up an action involving banks and other major corporations.

"Going to be lots of fun, this time kiddies. And there's a bit of job security. We want you to set up a structure so that there's not just one big party where we come in for the buzzkill. We want something we can come back to over and over again. This is about long term, how these fucking spider monkeys organise themselves, what their cute little values are, what goes on in their cute little spider monkey brains when they decide they're going to turn the country into a big fucking Glastonbury organic piss-and-pussy-juice-love-puddle. No offence intended, Martha my dear."

When we got back to London, I immediately scoured the internet for what Blackbird might not have been telling us. Our story was big and the media was pushing. Toby Montreaux had been on good form for the six weeks we'd been away. His first story was almost embarrassing:

> *"...A group of brave and committed young people with no agenda beyond the salvation of a planet from a culture that despises it. Their inevitably doomed heroic task was to make that destruction plain to us all, and by the look of Twitter, they've succeeded. I don't entirely condone their methods, such tactics often can be reduced to so much theatrics by the rightwing carnival barkers, but sometimes a population has to be shocked into action. I know I was shocked that day when I watched that martyred cetacean crashing to the ground from the top of one of our defunct temples to the cult of cheap energy and cheap lives..."*

As Blackbird told us on the ride back to London we were always referred to as having "gone to ground" in the stories. "Police believe the ringleaders may have a network of safe houses across the country". "That's not your story though, it's 'the mean ol' bill was sodomising us with Brigton rock and wotsits, sir..."Once we got settled in the new squat, a place on Mare Street that had been seized from some people who'd set up some kind of illegal bike repair shop, he told us, we were to tell anyone who would listen that we'd been in solitary confinement for the last six weeks and that we'd fought for our sanity, etc., etc., and that now we were, if anything, more committed to our ideals. The police couldn't break us. Never! Might even allude that the methods of interrogation weren't entirely Geneva compliant, if you know what I mean, Spanxy boy; ounce of prevention, innit?

The stories kept coming:
"More than 200 arrests..."
"The police claim to have disrupted seven highly sophisticated independent networks of what they refer to as *domestic extremism*. Commissioner Donald Justice was quoted as saying "Its going to be a long time before we have the full picture, but I think we're making headway in tackling a serious threat to the British way of life."

As I expected, as soon as I checked my mobile, dozens of messages from Toby Montreaux bleeped and rattled to life. "I'm out. I think I can tell my story now," I texted.
Two seconds later he wrote: "Come by the offices today. I'll be there."
I cycled up to King's Cross where the newspaper's HQ was. On the way I wondered if I should just pull the plug there and then, if I should just tell Toby Montreaux the whole story and finish it. But then I thought about the pact we'd made at Dove Cottage, that we rose or fell as a group not as any one individual. No, I decided as I chained up by the canal, I'd wait and I'd give Toby Montreaux the story he was looking for.

This was the story:

Activists Claim Harsh Treatment During Confinement

A group of activists detained following the high profile "Whale Drop" incident at the Battersea Power Station nearly two months ago have spoken for the first time about their captivity. An activist who refers to himself as "Spanx" contacted the Guardian yesterday to claim he was held in a British prison unit in solitary confinement, conditions amounting to torture.

"They put us in the wagon and I thought we'd be heading to Scrubs or Pentonville or something, but they just kept driving. Before we knew what happened we were outside of London altogether." *Spanx detailed a number of accusations, including sleep deprivation, deliberate extended isolation followed by periods of harsh interrogation.* *"All we were trying to do was raise awareness of the environmental consequences of our current economic and social system. It's a tradition that stretches back to the Magna Carta. We were treated like, I don't know, like al-Qaeda or something."* *The police have not responded to requests for information about the accusations nor about the claims of detention facilities in the Lake District.*

Asked whether the experience would deter him from engaging in future actions, Spanx stated that it would only make him more committed to exposing what he perceives to be injustices. Allegations of racial harassment have also been made against one of the arresting officers, Seargent Shane Warden.

After I left Toby Montreaux, I knew there was one more trip I had to make now that I was back in civilisation, or "snivelisation" as some distant part of my brain began calling it after the term Tomrade had used one night when we were up late listening to Crass albums. It was a trip I was dreading, but one I knew I had to make. It was also the journey I wanted to make most of all, the journey to Psyche's place. I read her emails in a cafe across from the Guardian offices. Each one pulled my heart, my mind, my entire being in different directions. The first was long and rambling.

"Dear Spanx,

I know they took you in. They got me, too, but they only held me for a few hours. I don't know where you are now, but I wanted to tell you how amazing you are. I've never met anyone like you. You're like some character from my high school dreams come to life! I know that sounds kind of weird, but I just think that it's best to be open with you and tell you how I feel. I'm not someone who's into the whole one-guy-one-woman thing--remember we talked about the whole 'ethical non-monogamy' thing back in Newquay, but I just ache to be around you now, and knowing you're probably banged up in some horrible prison just makes me want to cry and scream at the same time! Spanx, what we did, what *you* did, was amazing. At first, I admit it, I didn't trust you, I thought you were just trying to hook up for the night, but then when you showed me that lorry, I knew I was involved with someone who would change my life forever. I can't even find the words to describe what it was like at Whalerise. It was like something totally new had happened in the world, like a boundary between reality and dream had been breached, like you woke up one morning with wings or discovered that people gave each other flowers instead of money, but it was also like a ritual from the deep past. I studied tribal societies of Latin America at uni and one of the groups, a tribe in Peru had a ritual called the Ceremony of the Flying Whale in which the whole tribe would drink a special beer brewed with ayahuasca and the shaman would perform in a costume that was understood to make him the whale that gave birth to the universe, which was part of their mythology, too, I wish I could tell it to you now, to whisper it in your ear as you're sitting in that cell wherever you are! I felt like that day, Whalerise, was the birth of a new universe for me, a new self, and you helped give birth to that self, Spanx. I mean, I don't want to sound all weird again, but it's kind of like you're my mother. I hope you see that in the way it's intended, in the best possible way. Spanx, I love you. I want to be yours, for a while at least, to learn from you to be taught by you, to see your bravery, to comfort you when the world hurts you, to give you the strength to rise again

and face them all down, and for me to develop that same courage and creativity beside you! Oh, god! I've probably scared you off, but I had to say it. I'm pressing send!
<3, <3, <3, ,£, <3,
Psyche

The next email was just explaining that the symbol ",£" had been intended as another heart but she was "stoned and got the shift thing wrong". Then she sent me other emails, once she learned of my "situation" and those are too personal to share with anyone. They're some of the most precious documents I'd ever read in my life then and they still are now, despite everything. Then, after weeks went by I noticed a change. She wrote that the police kept coming by her place and asking her loads of questions. I can't tell you how much I hated the force after reading that message. The emails and texts became more matter of fact and the last one was wishing me luck and saying that if I wanted her, she'd always be waiting for me. That it was a promise.

She said she was living in a shared place off Powerscroft Road now, "Drop by anytime". I sent a text message "Is this anytime?" She replied almost before I remembered pressing send.
"Yes. Where are you?"
"Outside."
I saw a curtain twitch and then, again, in what seemed like less than a second, she was at the door She took a step back and I took a step in. She was wearing an oversized SOAS T-shirt and she had on a pair of tracksuit bottoms. She wasn't wearing any shoes. Her eyes filled with tears and she jumped into my arms.
"Take me to my room," she said.
"I don't know where it is,"
"Oh, shit, yeah," she said and stood back on the floor. "Come on."
Afterward she rolled over and lay on top of me. She arched her back up so she could look in my eyes.
"I thought you were gone, or that by the time you got back, you'd still be gone, you know? Like they'd have gotten to

you."
"I do know. You kept me sane, Psyche, even though you didn't know it."

I'd never said anything so sentimental in my life, in fact it was like my mouth formed the words without my brain knowing, as if my feelings were beyond the control of my logical brain. I kissed her and I told her that I was planning something else. Something much bigger than Whalerise.
"Spanx, I don't know."
"No, I know it's crazy. I know it's like so crazy it's actually insane, but I have to go through with this."
"Spanx, I've known a lot of guys who've had to deal with the feds. They get taken in for a night or a week or something and they come out saying 'this won't change me' or whatever, but it does change them, some it makes crazy, they're like 'I've got to prove myself' now, 'I've got to show them they can't get to me, they can't fuck with my head', but when people start thinking like that, they've *already* gotten into their heads. There's like literally a cop in their head, or a cop that kind of hovers over them staring straight into their eyes like a tractor beam or something," she stared straight into my eyes, playfully at first, silly grin and everything but then it was serious, like she was trying to show me that she could see 'they'd gotten to me'. I knew I had no choice then, I had to tell her the truth. The truth I feared more than anything.
"Psyche, I've got something to tell you. I've never known how to tell you this before, but I've wanted to tell you this since the first time I met you. It's true. I've felt like a fraud the whole time I've known you, but I have to tell you the truth now. It may...it may be the end of everything, but you have to know."
" Spanx, I want to hear anything you have to tell me. It won't change the way I feel."
I held my breath for a long time, I looked into the bottomlessness of her eyes, the careless way her hair slipped into her eyes and how she blew it back into place, how she lazily traced patterns on my side as she propped her head up so she could look

straight into my eyes, so that she could take in everything I was saying...

"Psyche," I said, tears were little electric pulses prickling at the corners of my eyes, "I have to tell you the truth."

"What is it, Spanx? You can tell me anything."

"I love you Psyche."

It was true.

Chapter X: The Plan

That night I called a general assembly at the squat. I told them that Psyche would be a part of things now, that we could trust her with anything except the one thing she probably would have most wanted to know. The Sneakies were sceptical.
"We don't need to be letting people in at this moment, especially this moment."
"I'm telling you, she's one of us now."
"Who we are isn't the problem. It's who we *were*. I think you can see that plainly enough.
"I do."
"Then you have to tell her at some point."
"I know I do, but if we told her now it would only confuse her, and she might think she can't trust us; that it's all some kind of trap. Look, let's just get through this. We have to burn the ships. This next operation has to be something from which there's no turning back. We're drawing the line. After today, we'll never be police again."
Everyone voted and it passed, just: we'd bring Psyche into the operation, but what was the operation?
The operational materials the office had given us suggested a series of invasions of offices in the city. We'd sit down, chain ourselves to something and wait for the police to come and hope something kicked off between the people we'd have with us and the staff or the police. It was, from their perspective, which in some ways was still my perspective, even then, a clever plan. Minimal risk to police, maximal visibility, the prospect of large scale arrests. They'd tip to offices beforehand, of course, then Bob's your uncle, everyone's happy, well, except for the people who aren't supposed to be. But I had other ideas.

We had to do some damage this time. This wasn't going to be an operation to "raise visibility" this was going to have some teeth. Sneaky Pete was the first to suggest a hack. I hadn't even been thinking along those lines, I guess I'm old school, but then it hit me. Yes, we'd hack. We'd hack the bloody City to pieces. We'd find the worst of the worst corporate criminals and we'd shine a little daylight on to their black magic.

We decided to hack into the Brewley Brothers Bank's internal server and send all the company emails to Toby Montreaux and friends. Peter had been working financial crime a few months before he was transferred and he said he knew it would be worth our time. "It's not going to be so much a 'shit hits the fan' moment as a 'diarrhea hits the wind turbine' moment."

"There are going to be envelope issues," Blackbird said, "we're hoping to bring a load of these fuckers, and the ecosystems their body hair hosts, to trial over the next eight weeks. We're going to need your charming and persuasive bottoms on the stand so we can nail their's to the floor of a cell."
"As us?"
"As bloody Spanx and his crew under pain of perjury fighting for his cause without shame, of course."
"When will you need us?"
"By the time I've changed the Observer pages under my cat's shit three times, you'll need to have this thing wrapped up."
"I think that's doable."

Chapter: Break

I won't pretend I wasn't dealing with a lot of issues. I was drinking. I was on drugs. I wasn't sleeping. I was having panic attacks that could only be controlled by locking myself in a quiet space in complete darkness and singing "Three Little Birds" by Bob Marley out loud. I was occasionally ramming people on my bike if they got in bike lanes. Plus, I was still trying to find a way to make my other confession to Psyche. I knew I'd waited too long, but every time I looked at her and got ready to tell her the truth, I came back to earth, I wasn't a demiurge channeling the fundamental forces of the universe, I was just a terrified little boy who knows he's done something unspeakable and therefore can't allow himself to speak about it even to himself. I was in denial. I kind of had to be, how could I admit that I had been a cop, looking into Psyche's eyes in the morning, directing the group in the afternoon, emailing Toby Montreaux after half a bottle of wine and some Xanax at the end of the day, how could I admit that as far as the world was concerned, I was still a cop? I'd learned the final secret of spying: the most important lies are the ones you tell yourself. I told myself very good lies.

There were other lies though, which were becoming a problem. Despite the best efforts of my employers, Professor Jonah Higgins of CEFAS wasn't going away. Every few days an article would appear in the *Independent* or *Guardian* saying something like "Questions Persist about Biologist's Arrest". Blackbird told me a bit about the backstory, but Toby told me more.
"It seems the good professor, your alter ego, Mr. Spanx, was arrested shortly *before* your operation, not, as every sensible person assumed, after. Now the police told us rather a different story. So there's only one real conclusion I can come to on that."
"Which is?"
"The police knew all about it, and they wanted it to happen."
"That's insane."
"I know. It's bloody madness. I don't have the whole picture yet, but it's the only thing that can be true. I expect you've read your Sherlock Holmes, Spanx? When you eliminate the

impossible..."
"So they knew..."
"And our friend Professor Higgins has had quite a bit of trouble from the police since, some rubbish about indecent images on his computer which faded away like the darling buds of May. Higgins is pleasantly paranoid, it turns out, he backed up his entire hard drive the day the police arrested him the first time. So he had a record of everything that was there, and everything that wasn't there. Very clever. Seems he knew what was coming somehow, but my question is how."
"They must have had him in their sights for a long time before. Maybe he's up to something of his own. Like real spying, the Russians or something?"
"Maybe. Look, Spanx, I'm not going to pretend to tell you about activism, you know a lot more than I do about the day to day, but I think you should be careful, because quite often, and there's a history of this sort of thing stretching way back, often the police will actually plant someone in an organisation like yours."
"I know that sort of thing happens, but I've known Lilith and Tank and Peter and Gavin forever, if they were feds..."
"No, I don't doubt you've known them, but the question, for me, is who might they have been before they were Lilith and Tank and Peter and Gavin. Now, relax, just relax, I don't mean literally like they're using assumed names and all that TV codswallop, I mean in terms of their biographies. Perhaps they weren't always involved in activist work. I could take a look if you'd like me to."
"No thanks, Toby, I think there are enough spies out there as it is."
"A spy? *Moi*? I'm a journalist."

Gavin knocked on my door. Psyche was showing me a few guitar chords. I was making a barred D-minor at the time.
"We're going to teach you to sing yet, Spanx."
"Uh, Spanx, I think you need to see this."
Gavin opened showed me a file on one of the hard drives he'd hacked. What he showed me was unbelievable.

"It's something like a database of all the "off-the-books" transactions they've been involved with over the last, what is it, three years. It's like looking at Satan's diary."
He was right. The document showed every kind of corporate abuse, sanctions busting, weapons dealing, rate fixing, all spelled out in forensic detail, dates, times, notes:

"Backchannel FIJI agreed to route payments through Sark."
"21/5/2010: Contact SAID ordered coffee and croissant, invoice attached. Concerns regarding chartering ship for delivery of payload. Has details for contact in Yangon for shipment through to DRC."
"Here's a meeting with...it can't be..."
Gavin showed me the name of a former Prime Minister. Apparently he'd met with high level officials at the bank and set up an account from which an associate in Khazakhstan frequently made withdrawls.
"I didn't even know they had cash machines in Khazakhstan."
"Well they do. They're called 'British banks'. And look, they've got stuff about fucking around with the Baltic Dry Index, markets, ratings agencies, the lot. Check this out. It's sort of beautiful and terrifying"
He pointed to a section of an email where the officials of the bank discuss laundering money made off an arms deal in Rwanda by funding albums by Skrillex.
"Fucking explains everything."
"This is massive. If we were to put this out there, then everything..."
"Yeah, Spanx, everything, and every one."
We were almost giddy then. We hugged each other. I distinctly remember jumping for joy, something I'd never done before or since. When I came down from my euphoria, I kissed Psyche. She held my head between her hands looked into my eyes and said it was the proudest she'd ever been of anyone. God, to have that feeling again...

The question now was what to do with the material we'd found. Sure, there were a lot of emails which were bad enough on the company's internal server. The usual stuff about rate

rigging, shell companies and the like, but the motherload was that database. I thought immediately about giving it to Toby Montreaux, but Tank persuaded me to stop.
"After all this shit, I want to catch me some coppers. You know that lot, us, are backhanding somewhere along this. Gavin you were a narc, too. You know that shit doesn't just disappear when it 'just disappears'"
"He's right, Spanx, they'll be laundering somewhere, but the thing is, what if they're not doing it at Brewleys', we just happen to be into them but if we were to maybe do some snooping we could really make some noise in the offices."
"If this stuff gets out there too soon, a hundred databases just like it will disappear in seconds."
"But if it doesn't, then it doesn't."
I loved the idea, but somehow it felt like time was crucial, like if we left it too long, Brewley's would catch us snooping and it would be game over. We agreed to make a decision first thing in the morning, publish, or dig deeper

It was six thirty AM. My phone was ringing. Toby Montreaux told me he'd done some digging himself. He'd found something he knew I needed to see. It wouldn't be good news, but it was very important and it would save trouble down the line. Maybe for the whole country, he added. He'd obviously found something, but I wasn't sure what, no matter what it was, he was right, it wouldn't be good news, but, I thought, if Operation HAIRCUT, as we'd christened the Brewleys op, was going to have any hope of success, then I had to know what he knew And so, feeling a kind of sting with every pump of my legs, I cycled down to King's Cross to meet Toby.

He was sitting at his desk with three computers humming. Laptops were also glowing menacingly from each of his knees.
"Spanx, I'm glad you could come. You're going to want to sit down."
I looked around but there didn't seem to be a chair anywhere, so I leaned against his desk and he started opening email accounts.

"This is big, Spanx, very big."
It seemed my organisation was being targeted by the police. In fact, the targeting had gone on for a long time.
"From what I've been able to put together, they've been watching you ever since Whalerise. Obviously that's not going to be a terrible surprise to you. But I've found something else, and I think that might be a bit more disturbing. He showed me an email. It was headed Project SUBFIASCO.

> CORVUS
> corvus@fiascosub.gov.uk
> to: deepestdarkest@fiascosub.gov.uk
> Replying to your concerns of prev, Operative EGO in place at BASE1. Will report status as operation progresses.

So it wasn't serious. What he showed me looked like an internal report about us being reestablished in the new squat. The dates suggested it was a routine check up, some variation on Blokey McBloke parking across the road and sitting there until either one of us came home or his bladder gave out. I wondered which one of us was EGO in the internal reports. I assumed it was me of course. Inside, I was singing, outside, I had to maintain an air of agitation. What Toby showed me next was the end of any song I might have been singing.

"As you can see, they've got someone inside. I made a few calls and I managed to turn this up. It's a picture of this 'EGO' person." He handed me an envelope. It was an operative profile on EGO. Paperclipped to the upper righthand corner was a passport sized image from a mugshot. It was Psyche. I could see Toby Montreaux's very serious face talking to me but I couldn't hear a word. The sound of my entire life imploding crashing to earth like the whale itself on Whalerise, smashing into a gelatinous mess, that was too deafening for anything else to get in.
"Spanx, *Spanx*, did you get that? Did you hear what I was saying?"

"Sorry, Toby, I kind of...drifted. It's just kind of a shock, you know."
"I understand Spanx, but this bit is critical. This woman, EGO, she's supposed to lure you into some kind of a masterplan of theirs. They've apparently coordinated with the blokes down a Brewley Brothers' Bank if you can believe it. The whole thing strikes me as absolutely bonkers, but it looks like--and I'll just bring it up on the screen here--they've set up some kind of phony database full of junk data that they want you to break into, presumably so they can arrest you before you do any real damage to Brewley Brothers. If you should be planning to do any damage to Brewley Brothers that is."

The sound of crashing returned to my ears. It was a symphony of smashing and grinding, all the atoms in the universe were careering into each other and exploding, spraying atom juice all over Toby's responsibly-sourced Icelandic jumper. It was an armageddon but I was the only person experiencing it. I remember Toby asking if I was with him again, but at some point, almost involuntarily, I stood up and started making my way to the door.
"Spanx? Spanx come back...SPANX!"
That was the last thing I heard Toby say. I was on my bike seconds later, pushing with every ounce of energy in my body. I was moving up Clerkenwell Road but I had no idea where I was going.

Chapter: XI After the End of the World

This is the thing about a secret, you never know if you're the only one who knows it. I nearly went arse-over-tit when I skidded into a pub off Leonard Street to think exactly what the fuck it was I should do now. What kept coming back to me was that terrible little puzzle. So now I knew that Psyche was a spy, but I didn't know if I was the only one who knew it. My mind was a paranoia factory, producing ever more baroque variations on the initial vintage of panic I felt when I saw her mugshot on the cover of Toby Montreaux's report. So Psyche was a cop, but what about the others, what about the "ex-cops" I'd made my bargain with? Were they ex-cops, or was I the only one who'd really crossed over that night in Dove Cottage? Was all of that an op to trap me? Or to trap all of us? Then there was Toby Montreaux, could I actually trust him? I knew he'd written some critical stuff about the police, but maybe he'd written it just so he'd look like he was independent. Maybe he was police too. Deep, deep, deep, responsibly-sourced Scandinavian cover. The words he said when he presented it, "someone inside". Inside where? Inside the department? Inside the squat? Inside Blackbird's frontal lobe? Between panic attacks and pints what I kept asking was whether the "someone inside" who gave Toby the files was someone who wanted me, for their own reasons, to find out about the whole little party. Was I supposed to know that they knew, and once they knew I knew, then they probably knew something else too. But what? It was a terrible feeling the kind I'm sure many people felt because of me as I look back on the whole sorry chapter of my sorry life. I decided then that I couldn't trust anyone. And in taking that decision, I knew what I had to do.

"Spanx! I haven't seen you for a while."
"Tomrade. How's life."
"You know, same shit different executive pay."
"Good ol' Tomrade. Smoke?"
"Like a free range salmon, mammon."
We went up to Tomrade's lair and he lit a bowl and turned on "Sugar Man". I normally wouldn't have inhaled, it interfered with my sense of balance on the bike, but today, I really didn't

care. If I died then I died, it didn't matter. With that morbid thought hovering above the remnants of stoner-small talk, I asked Tomrade if he could cue up "Send Me On My Way" by Rusted Root. Quietly it had become one of my favourite songs over the last year and I could think of no better way to sum up what waited for me that evening.
"Mr. Fuckin' Retro bitch. *I am a 90s bitch*," he said scrolling the playlist.
"Tomrade, you remember when I got out of the copshop?"
"Not much of it, mate, no. That was one unrememberable night."
"You do remember what I gave you the morning after, don't you?"
"Other than a cotton-mouth blow job, bro? I still got the callouses."
"Tomrade, I'm serious."
"So am I bro, you want to see? No, seriously, yeah, of-fucking-course I remember."
"Today's the day."
"Holy sugar, batman."
Tomrade took down a pile of LPs from his record shelf and pulled out the object I'd referred to as my "stash".
"Special occasion man. If I'd'a' known I'd'a' bought something other than fucking Kronenberg. Cava or some shit."
"Thanks Tomrade."
"What the dilly, bro? You're not going to give ol' Tomrade a taste? That's a little bit finance if you ask me."
"It's not that kind of stash, Tomrade."
"No?"
"No. Thanks, for watching it man. We're best stock dividends forever man," I said. We hugged and I gave him roll of ten £50 notes I'd taken from the wall-safe that morning for when I went to Toby's office.
"Buy some Panama Red with it."
"You better Lloyd's TSB it. You can't stick and stay? You sure, bro?"
"It's a little unfinished business with an old connection, Tomrade. I can't."

"Okay, okay, stop right there, Spanxy, or I'm going to lose my status as a civilian."
He walked me to the door and as I was unchaining my bike he waved to me slowly. The way you wave when you know you won't see someone again.
"*...lose my status as a civilian...*"
Tomrade? Was he police too? When I checked the stash box in the alley behind the squat I confirmed that he wasn't. Shooter and magazine in tact. Time for my "business meeting."

I walked into the squat as calmly as possible. I made my way up the stairs to our individual rooms. Nobody in mine. Nobody in Tank's. Lilith, out to lunch. No Peter. Only Gavin tapping away at his computer from behind a closed door. I decided to be polite. I knocked. Gavin opened his door.
"Hey mate, I've got a lot of stuff you'll want to see."
"Yeah, well, I've got something you should probably see too."
I pulled out the glock and told him to stand against the opposite wall.
"What the fuck, Spanx, is this, was this all some kind of..."
"Just shut up while I frisk you."
I ran my hands over him and checked him for weapons or listening devices. I realised midway through that it was all probably pointless. They'd have been installing bugs while they kept us up in the Lake District. I dragged him downstairs and we went out into the garden. I told him to sit in the lawn chair opposite me as I walked out into the garden, keeping my gun low so that any cameras wouldn't pick it up. Surely there would be cameras.
"Can I ask what all this is?"
"I don't know what it is yet. But I know we're in trouble."
"I should bloody think so," he said, halfway to tears as he pointed to me.
"That database, what do you know about it?"
"You mean meta? I haven't even considered meta, I've just been digging through what it tells us in the transactions, checking dates and that."

"What's the IP address?"
"We can check."
"Not now."
"Spanx, what's happening. This is a *madness*! Where did you get that gu--"
I put my finger to my lips. In the time it took, I realised how doomed I was. No matter what I said to Gavin, the second I left, he would be on the phone to Tank, who'd be on the phone to Martha who'd be on the phone to Sneaky Pete and all of them would be on the phone to Blackbird because he'd be listening to every bloody one of them on their bugged phones. Looking across the garden at Gavin, I knew what would happen next. I knew in fifteen minutes time, after he told me whatever he was going to tell me, he was going to be dead. I'd take him into the storage cellar of the squat, tie him up, kick some of the boxes around to disguise the sound and I'd shoot him and that would be that. I would be a fugitive. As I listened to him talk, it was all I could think about. I could see his face and his mouth moving but all I could see was a skull with words streaming out of it. I tried not to let it blot out everything he was saying but it did. Dead man walking. Dead man sitting. Dead man talking. Dead man sweating. Dead man scratching his ear...

What saved Gavin was the sound of the front door clattering open and Tank struggling with his bike.
"Don't move."
"Spanx, he's just..."
"I said don't fucking move."
"This the mad hacker's tea party going on back here? Oh, shit, white boy with a gun. Time for me to check on my casserole."
"Raymond, don't move. I don't want to shoot you."
"Then we've got something in common. We can build on that, my brother."
"He's lost it Raymond, I think he's working for Blackbird."
"I need to know what you know about the Brewley affair."
"I don't pry."
"I learned a nasty little secret."
"Oh yeah?"

"Raymond don't fuck with him."
"Oh yeah. You know what it is?"
"Not related to Ryan Giggs is it? Can at least make some cash before you get sectioned."
"No, it's not related to Ryan Giggs. It's that there's a wolf in the hen house."
"You mean a fox."
"I mean 'fuck off'. I mean there's someone here who's not on Operation WORDSWORTH, that person is on a different operation, an operation called SUBFIASCO. Mean anything to you?"
"Is it even a word?"
"It's not a word, it's an understatement. I'm tired of this shit."
"Good, 'cause I need a shower, Gavin, come on. I'll teach you how to floss."
"They know everything. Blackbird, base, Tunnel Ops, they set up that account with Brewleys'.
Tank stopped. "I think I need to sit down," he said.
"You know this, Spanx," Gavin sked
"Read for yourself."
I showed them the files Toby Montreaux had sent me. Read for yourself.

To: brewcrew1@brewleysmgmt.net
From: deepestdarkest@fiascosub.gov.uk

Mr. Carter,

Thank you for being so understanding about our little predicament. It was a pleasure to speak with you in person. Following from our conversation, we've begun to implement the agreement. We'll have one of our IT orcs rolling around your way later this afternoon to set up the DB. The question remains as to how far you want to get involved in the operational element. We feel we could always use support, but there are issues of deniability which you may need to consider. Things have been more complex than we'd hoped since some rather leaky shit has hit a certain high-powered fan called the internet. Cue the ministers ringing up with rhetorical questions, "Perhaps I'm old fashioned but I do find it a bit odd that we're now paying the police to break the law" and that type of thing. What rock that old boy was scraped out from is a question even our best and brightest can't solve.

We should be out of your hair by the weekend and thank you again. If your offer to visit that spa still stands, I can only say I have gotten a little weary of having to go to Soho for a decent massage.

keep the faith and hello to your brother,
Justice

"So you think this whole thing is a--"
"The only thing I do know is this."
I handed them the file with Psyche's picture on it.
No one said anything.
"Do you know where she is now?"
"Well, she told me she was going to work, but fuck knows, could mean she's giving Blackbird one of his special massages."
"What do we do now?"
What do we do now? It was a question that had no answer. What do you do once you know everything you've worked for has all been a complete and utter sham. We'd been duped and no doubt they had a fine fate waiting for us, the cells, solitary, a dingy dining room full of lags whispering to each other that we were once police, planning a thousand grisly undoings for us. What do we do now? The few seconds since Gavin had asked the question expanded into vast wastes of space-time. Any moment there would be a rush and the front door would come splintering in and they'd have us facedown, guns blazing, itching to take us out. And every second it didn't happen took us deeper into the trap, deeper into some Tunnel Op inevitability. We only had one card to play, and if something kept Blackbird hovering, I knew it could only be one thing:

the bowel-shredding knowledge that if they nailed us, they might just be nailing themselves. That minister, whoever he was who came round asking about the police committing crimes, what would he think of a police operation to raid a rogue police cell? Heads would roll. In Britain, curtains twitch on every avenue, everyone from the PM to the tarot readers spent their days wondering what the neighbours think. Will it look bad? How could it look worse? With that realisation, I think I finally broke the code, Blackbird's game wasn't to do us over, it was to do nothing, and to keep us from doing anything, to keep this mad little police drama he'd contrived running for as long as possible without ever letting the season-ending cliffhanger take place. There would never be another Whalerise, he'd make sure of that, with Psyche's help, but there would always be someone somewhere to spy on, and of course, there would also always be someone to spy on the spies. It was our job to live, and to roll one aborted operation after another up the hill of time until retirement, and that would be enough. What were we going to do now? The only thing we could do. "We wait."

I explained the situation as I saw it to Raymond and Gavin and they agreed that we'd have to just play our assigned roles until we found a way to get free. That night when Psyche came home, I pretended to be too drunk to talk to her. She got undressed and came to bed as I pretended to be asleep. She curled up and twined her leg around mine like any other night. I was doing everything I could to maintain the kind of regular breathing pattern that would indicate that I was sleeping, but it was almost impossible, the sheer exhaustion of it. I felt a tear leak out and spill down onto the pillow. I felt Psyche's body slacken and knew she was asleep. Me, I would be up for hours, contemplating how easy it would have to become to lie to her a second time, not about my secrets, but about hers.

Psyche left early the next morning because, she said, she had a "doctor's appointment". I wondered if that was some kind of contemptuous code she had with

herself for her appointments with Blackbird. I kissed her good-bye and said "Nothing serious, is it babe?" "Is anything serious?" She said and she got on my bicycle.
I watched her pedal down toward Mare Street and immediately my mind switched back to the pandemonium it had been before. No, I thought, I wasn't going to let her go to her little meeting. I was going to stay in control of our strange little menage a trois. I texted Blackbird, "Meeting? ASAP? Issues." If she was off to meet Blackbird, well, maybe he just wouldn't be there. I got a text back a few minutes later.
"Issues? What kind of issues? Finally discover you're a pathetic woman trapped in a pathetic man's body? 10.15 Westminster Bridge."

As I rode the tube to see Blackbird, it suddenly occurred to me that I actually didn't have anything to talk to him about. I couldn't just bloody turn up, smile and tell him I just wanted to say 'hi'. I had to come up with something, something he didn't know about already that was. That was when, halfway between Westminster and St. James Park, I dreamed up Operation DAMASCUS ROAD. When I got to Westminster there were tour groups everywhere, Dutch school children were hurrying past me and shouting to each other. A group of Korean tourists were following a man in a bowler hat and a red umbrella. French schoolgirls and bloated Americans were dutifully taking holiday snaps of Parliament or themselves in the shadow of Churchill's statue. As I made my way to the bridge, one of the Americans stopped me.
"Hey buddy, any chance you know where the Abraham Lincoln statue is here? You know, ol' Honest Abe? You guys call him that over here?"
"It's back there," I said pointing past a clutch of protesters huddled on the pavement by the grass.
"Thanks, buddy. Tally ho. That means 'good-bye', right?"
"More or less."
"Thanks, fella."
So was he one of Blackbird's people? I had no idea anymore. Was "Lincoln" some kind of code word? Why wouldn't it be?

The sky was fermenting, rain bleeding from the black rags of clouds. I came to the bridge and I could see Blackbird there looking mildly annoyed beneath his umbrella. I nodded hello to him.
"Going to confess you've secretly harboured amourous desires for me the whole time you've been in the department? Tell me that's what it is, I've got a bet with Philately Frank down in Tunnel Ops."
"Of course, sir. I love you."
"Thought so. Now, do you want to start making sense or should we adjourn to Hampstead Heath?"
"I couldn't talk to the others about this. I think we're spinning our wheels on the present project, sir."
"Well, well, well. You always were an ambitious boy. They tell me you started wanking as soon as the doctor spanked your arse. Boy who knew what he wanted from life."
"I'm tired of these slap on the wrist operations, sir. No, uh, pun intended. With respect, I just think the best thing we can hope for from this thing is just a few more names in the data base and a few cheek swabs no one will want in a few years' time anyway. I'd like to actually take some people down, sir. For a long time."
"Sounds as pleasant as sherbet after a blow job. Tell me more."
"I want to stage a robbery."
"Now you're fucking enunciating. Robberies are good."
"But I want to dress it up, make it seem real, pull in a lot of rags and bones from the squats."
"Any place in particular or just a good old smash and grab? Some things are easier to explain operationally than others, my son."
"Brewleys' Bank."
"That's a novel idea."
"We want to make it high profile. We're thinking central London, Hanover Square."
"And there'll be affray? I like affray"
"It could get violent."
"I like violence."

I gave Blackbird a date for the operation and the basic logistics, time of day, amount of personnel, where "our" guys would be throughout, all from the notes I'd scribbled on the back of an envelope on the escalator at Westminster station. "All looks congenial, but I'll have to make a few calls."

"Understandable, sir."

"Paranoia doesn't go as far as it used to since the last jobbie you lot pulled. M'fucking learned reptillians are asking all kinds of annoying questions about the circumstances of your ingress into Battersea, needless to say the megafauna of our little food chain have to know as little as possible."

"Understood, sir."

Blackbird gave me a quick arch of his eyebrows and disappeared into the square between the barriers, police and tourists. I stood on Westminster Bridge, the sky low with rain, the cabs and cyclists thrashing out their daily battle along the assault course of construction orange. The city in the late afternoon, in the misery of rain and traffic, even the Thames seemed crowded and overwhelmed, barges, the Tate ferry, the usual cruises, that amphibious duck-shaped boat-bus was slipping into the water like a massive ovary full of tourists. Everyone was wide awake, going about their business or the pretense of their business, or someone else's business, but in a way they were like the people in that Wordsworth poem, too: in a deep sleep, so still that it seemed the buildings too were drugged into catatonia. Their windows were glazed and drowsy and you couldn't see anything happening behind them. They were asleep to the world, to the violence and the suffering, to the methane chimneys spewing up from the tundra of the arctic. The mass die-offs besides. The rubbish island floating in the Pacific Ocean with all radioactive water from Fukashima. They were asleep to my little plot and anti-plot dance with Blackbird and the whole spy-vs-spy bollocks intelligence services go through to impress each other. As Blackbird and I had stood on the bridge and talked, Asian kids took selfies with Big Ben as the backdrop, lorries and double decker busses strained at the start and stop construction decreed, and the eternal juddering of the jackhammer, enough to wake the dead but not the living, that was London now and that was the world, alive only to the act of excluding what it didn't want to see, or couldn't withstand seeing.

I felt the weight of my jumper, I was getting very wet, so sodden it felt like it might drag me into a puddle and then into the sewer, then into the Thames where I'd just dissolve into all the vast ignorance pissed into the river every day by every one of us. I had to get inside. I had to get dry. So I stopped into a pub near parliament. Sky News was on, it was a report on acidification of the oceans. The expert suggested the ocean was becoming a massive carbon sink, and in the process, reefs were dying, fish populations declining, and, she said, "This is giving us a false sense of security as well. If temperatures drop, or even steady out, it looks like the process has slowed, when, of course nothing of the kind has happened." The people at the table next to me let out a chorus of cheers when their sausage and celeriac mash with wasabi arrived. *A false sense of security.*

When I came home that night, Psyche was in the living room on her laptop, headphones crackling, deep in thought. She didn't even notice me until I sat down.
"Mr. Spanx."
"How'd it go down at the doctor's?"
"Well, good news and bad news."
"Bad news?"
"Yeah, well, kinda depends on your outlook, really."
"Should I be worried?"
"It depends."
"On?"
"Well, Mr. Spanx, what do you think about babies?"
I was frozen, calcified. Earlier in the day the doctor wasn't even real, in an instant we were beyond doctors on to paediatricians.
"You're sure?"
"I'm sure. You know, I think, I think it happened on Whalerise, Spanx."
"You didn't tell me…"
"Well, I couldn't very well tell you could I. You were

somewhere else. But I've told you now. That's something, isn't it?"

"It is."

I looked into her eyes and saw myself; my face was upside down, contorted like the strata of the earth's crust after an earthquake, what emotion was I meaning to convey or to conceal? I had no idea, but I knew she'd told me the truth because there was some part of her they still hadn't gotten into and infected. And so I knew there was some part of her I could still count on. And, knowing that, I told her then and there. I told her the whole story. The story she already knew and the part she didn't know: There was to be a bank robbery at a Brewley Brothers Bank and that I knew who would be responsible for it.

"Spanx, I don't think you should do it."

"You're probably right. But it's about what I have to do because there's something else I have to tell you."

And that's when I told her the truth, the real truth, the truth about the operation, Operation CHSTERTON. I had to know what she would do, not what she would tell Blackbird, but what she would do sitting there in front of me. She was silent for a long time. I think she was shocked that I actually managed to tell her the truth. Or perhaps that I was capable of telling the truth about anything.

"Spanx, that's, wait, Spanx isn't your real name is it?"

"It's my name now, because it's who I am now."

She put her hands on the sides of my head and pulled me in so that I was staring her straight in the face.

"But who will you be? Who will you be tomorrow, and the day after that, and a month from now, and when Junior Spanx needs his boosters? Who will you be then? Do you know?"

"I don't think anyone knows."

"I'm supposed to trust you now? I'm supposed to put my life in your hands when you've shown how easy it is for you to deny that your own bloody hands belong to you," she'd paused on the word "bloody", she looked at her own hands, "These hands? These are 'Spanx's' hands. Don't know anything about it. Me? Pleased to meet you, call me 'Reggie'."

I couldn't say anything to her. She had a right to hate me, more than a right, an obligation even, to seek vengeance, to seek it in the worst and most damaging way. I couldn't hold her responsible for that. And so I continued to say nothing. I just sat across our kitchen table from her and waited for her to say something. I waited for her to say anything. Then, as the silence grew, I waited for her to say something else, and after an even longer stretch of silence, a silence that seemed deep enough to cover all the sound in the world, no sirens or kids in the street, no air circulating, nothing. I gave up waiting and knew that I didn't deserve an answer. I stood up. She made as if she wanted to keep me there with her but then she turned away again. I went up to our room and I lay in bed and cried. Somewhere in my head I kept hearing a voice, not my voice, but also not *not* my voice asking me over and over again, "whose tears are you crying?" Psyche came to the door. I tried to control myself but I couldn't stop the tears from coming. She climbed into bed with me and put her arms over me. I pulled her in. The voice was still speaking still interrogating me, whose tears are those? Whose tears are you crying? Then the answer came to me. They were Psyche's tears.

In the morning, I kissed her good-bye and began the implementation of Operation ANANAIS, the shadow of Operation DAMASCUS ROAD. Tank was to stay at the squat and "look after the herb garden", and to text me when and if Psyche left the house to tell Blackbird of my movements as she surely would. That she couldn't avoid, and I'm sure she knew I knew as much. I met The Sneakies in a bike repair shop cum café in Broadway Market. All around us, tattooed guys with beards struggled with tyres and tubes, one guy used his latte's spoon to wrench a flat from his rim. It was as noisy as it needed to be and as oblivious to the world beyond its own Brooks saddle as I could possibly have hoped. We drew up the plan. There was going to be a bank robbery, alright, but it was going to be a very special kind of robbery. Once we were sure of what we were doing, this is the manifesto we wrote..

People of Good Conscience,
Today, myself and a group of environmentalists have undertaken something we call Operation Damascus Road by means of which we hope to help society see what is directly before its eyes, yet is still too clearly hidden in plain sight to be visible. By the time you read this, we will have engaged in a direct action that will, in many ways resemble the phenomenon known historically as a "bank robbery".

In the wake of the massive state bailout of financial institutions in the autumn of 2009, it has since become clear through materials we hope to publish along with this manifesto that financial institutions, particularly the targeted bank, Brewley Brothers bank, have been systematically committing acts of robbery against the population of Great Britain and the world. We intend to reenact on a small (and much more personally risky) scale, the kind of operation they perform everyday on the citizenry at large from the safety of their offices armed not with guns and balaclavas but with keyboards and spreadsheets and bad ideas. In the year 2011 alone, Brewley Brothers were directly involved in three large scale transactions involving speculation in basic dietary staples (corn, sunflower seeds and quinoa), raising the prices for food throughout the world and contributing directly to uncountable deaths in the developing world, and, increasingly in our own undeveloping world.

Brewley was also involved in the warehousing of funds for dictators, warlords and other corrupt international actors, including knowingly abetting money laundering for the drug baron Boris Marron and maintaining several accounts connected to the regime in a West African state repeatedly implicated in large scale human rights abuses, and socially destructive "development" projects (a uranium mine and a railway project which displaced 353 families which are yet to be resettled, for more see this site: www. brewleybrotherswatch.org.uk). The bank also is estimated *to have made £7.3 billion on its investments involving the arms trade including deals with the usual suspects, Saudi, Colombia, and Bahrain as well as dealings with shadowy regimes like Kazakhstan, Kyrgyzstan, and Uzbekistan (and lots of other places you'd need more than Google Maps to find). They've also played a decisive role in investing in dangerous forms of genetically modified foods and organisms including a range of pigs intended to be sold as pets which were cross-bred with a primitive undersea organism called a "dinoflagellate" because of the dinoflagellate's bioluminescent properties. The chimera organisms created were unviable and died hideous deaths in their corporate laboratory cells (to watch the gruesome video for yourself, click here: www.stopkillingdinopigs.org.uk). They were also implicated in breaking UN sanctions regimes on three known occasions, one of which they were held responsible for in US courts to the tune of $240million. Brewleys also financed a bizarre weekend concert in Azerbaijan involving Sting, Jay-Z, Akon, Skrillex, and Don Henley (to see the video of Akon rapping with the dictator's wannabe pop-star daughter—with Sting accompanying the whole she-bang on the lute, click here: www.googooshkasux.tv). Your tax dollars at work. If their crimes weren't heinous enough, their music tastes would be. And who are the "they" behind Brewley Brothers' Bank? David and Thomas Carter, residents of the Turks and Caicos Islands tax haven, non-domiciled residents under British law. The brothers share legal oversight of Brewley. It seems have never met a theft they didn't like. Today, we are putting that to the test. The money that will be taken from Brewleys' vaults today will be anonymously donated to renewable energy projects and global peace initiatives. For their own protection and ours we will not name the organisations but we will manage the donations quietly and keep the responsible staff of the organisations in the dark so that they will never be forced to hand the money back to Brewleys' Bank or its corrupt ownership. We encourage all customers at Brewleys' to immediately withdraw their accounts in*

solidarity, and we hope that even those who choose not to do so will see the logical and moral purpose of our actions.
Peace, Solidarity and 22/7,
The 4.20 Blackbirds

That was yesterday evening. The file's timestamp says I stopped working on it at around 11.34. I showed it to Psyche. She told me she didn't want to look at it, that it would stress her out.
"I think it's important that you see it, that you understand where I'm coming from now."
"This is dangerous, Spanx."
She didn't say anything else, but I knew the danger she meant, the danger of having to discriminate between loyalties. Do you trust the man who betrayed you, or the man you're betraying, or the man to whom you've betrayed him? Do you trust yourself to decide? I asked her to read the manifesto again. She agreed and I set it in front of her. I saw a tear drop on the keyboard and seep between the keys as she scrolled through it.

I'm looking over that manifesto now. T-minus ten minutes from the beginning of Operation ANANIAS. Looking it over, I can only say one thing, and that's that it tells the truth. Well, it tells a version of the truth. The rest of this message should tell you the whole truth. That's all I've ever wanted, the only thing worth committing yourself to after so much lying. And this is the truth, as complete as I know it:

I'm sitting in an internet cafe in London on Mile End Road between a Chinese buffet restaurant called the Green Door and a biryani shop called Dynamo Grill. I'm watching the locals congregated on the pavement as a delivery man scuds up on his motorbike to pick up more egg fried rice to deliver to the offices in Canary Wharf for lunch break. It's sunny. There's a white gloss to everything that passes by, car windscreens, busses, the tops of shops across the street, the leaves on the big tree just in front of the shop. Across the street is the branch of Brewley Brothers where everything begins. In nine minutes we go in. All of us. Peter guarding the door, Tank and myself going in for the raid and Lilith driving getaway. Well, not all of us. Right now I'm about to send a text to Gavin. There it goes. He'll start walking down Conduit street now towards Hanover Square. He'll see Psyche sitting on a park bench there reading the newspaper and listening to headphones. He'll stand over her, she'll be covered by his shadow. She'll stand up and they'll walk together toward the branch of Brewley Brothers' Bank just next to the yacht management place. Blackbird and his people will be watching them go in, waiting for the others to turn up, but they never will. About the time Blackbird starts getting nervous Gavin and Psyche will still be calmly chatting about opening a joint account for their new arrival. When the bank manager asks for Gavin's passport, Blackbird will hear the first news of tweets of a bank robbery at Brewley Brothers and a manifesto being sent to the media claiming responsibility. He'll be sipping his tea and muttering to himself, swearing, "Fucking fuckers where the fuck… did they take the bloody northern line?" But that will all be in the future. In seven minutes' time, there should be an 8G8 security lorry pulling up outside the bank, at that point, I'll press send on this email and it will arrive in the inbox of Toby Montreaux. I've just dropped memory sticks confirming everything I've written here with full documentation into the post-box outside the massive post office on Whitechapel High Street. There's the 8G8 lorry now. My message has just been sent to Toby. And now I'm putting the finishing touches on this email to you, Psyche. I don't know what will happen in the next ten minutes, but I'm prepared for anything, God knows I've lived through everything already and been everyone. I don't know if I'll see you again, or what my name will be if I do. Take good care of our child, I know you will. I have no recommendations for a name, though William if it's a boy or Dorothy if it's a girl would look back to an important time in my life. Please know I've done this so that he or she will live in the kind of world where no one has to make the kind of choices we've made. The kind of choices the person you sleep next to can never know about.